Your Mind Redefined

Rediscover God's Plan for Health, Happiness, and Hope

Janet R. Leathem PMHNP, BC

ISBN: 1507822502
ISBN-13: 978-1507822500

DEDICATION

This book is dedicated to women around the world who need to know the truth about how to use their brain to influence their health—physically, emotionally, and spiritually, to become "a vessel of honor, sanctified and useful for the Master, prepared for every good work." (II Timothy 2:21)

I also dedicate this book to the memory of Dr. Mark Maxwell, my mentor and friend, who taught me to love women's reproductive psychiatry and care for women's emotional health across the lifespan. His impact on my life left an indelible mark that I will always remember.

CONTENTS

Introduction 1

Part I: The Brain - Key to Optimal Health 3

Chapter 1: Control Center for Emotions 8

Chapter 2: Seven Emotional Components of the Brain 19

Chapter 3: Five Skills to Develop Your Emotional Health 31

Chapter 4: Is Your Brain on Strike? 43

Chapter 5: Hormones - Fuel for Health 62

Chapter 6: Use Your Brain to Overcome Insomnia 84

Chapter 7: Diet, Exercise, & Supplements - What You Should Know 98

Chapter 8: Hope & Happiness - Spiritual Foundation for Health 120

Part II: Readings to Renew Your Mind & Restore Your Spirit 129

Cultivate the Fruit of the Spirit 129

Chapter 9: Love 131

Chapter 10: Joy 136

Chapter 11: Peace 140

Chapter 12: Patience 144

Chapter 13: Kindness 148

Chapter 14: Goodness (Generosity) 152

Chapter 15: Faith 156

Chapter 16: Gentleness 162

Chapter 17: Self-Control 166

Conclusion: Press On Towards the Goal 174

Appendices & References 176

ACKNOWLEDGEMENTS

I would like to acknowledge all the women I have cared for who have invited me into their lives to share their journey. Their experiences have taught me a great deal about how God designed the unique female brain and the intricate way that God has caused our body, mind, and spirit to work together in perfect harmony to promote health and wellness.

I acknowledge my mother, Doris Katherine Zimmer Johnsen, an amazing and Godly woman who taught me many of the principles discussed in this book. She went home to be with her Savior on December 11, 2008, but her legacy and influence lives on in my life and all those whom she touched.

I acknowledge my son, Jonathan Leathem, for his creative design and implementation of this book. Without his patience, knowledge, vision, and skill this project would not have reached completion. His ability to take a problem and turn it into an opportunity is awesome!

I also acknowledge Olivia Anderson, who tirelessly helped with the editing of this manuscript. Her creative comments and ideas helped to cement the concepts that I was trying to convey. Her skill as a word sculptress is greatly appreciated.

Finally, I give grateful thanks to my husband, David Leathem, for his assistance with proofreading and providing general feedback to help make the concepts presented more "readable." I thank my entire family, including my son, Jared Leathem, for their prayer support, patience, and love. Most of all, I thank the Lord Jesus Christ for giving me the opportunity to share with others some of the important principles of spiritual health taught in the Word of God.

INTRODUCTION

The brain is our body's most complex organ. Weighing only about three pounds, it controls our every thought and action by means of an intricate system of nerve fibers, chemical messengers, and hormones. Everything we know about the world and how we interpret it comes through our five senses of sight, sound, smell, taste, and touch. In fact, right now, your brain and nervous system are actively working to understand this sentence - just one example of how essential the brain is to every function of our waking and sleeping life.

However, our brain not only interprets the world, it uniquely customizes it as well. Our senses interpret the world around us in such a way that can either spark creativity, contentment, and hope, or create anxiety, frustration, anger, and depression. That is why David in Psalm 34:8 could say, "Oh, taste and see that the Lord is good; Blessed (happy) is the man who trusts in Him!" The Apostle Paul also tells us that "the peace of God . . .will *guard your hearts and minds through Christ Jesus,*" (Philippians 4:7). Our senses are the gateway to our mind and ultimately our emotional, spiritual, and even our physical health. While neurons and genes all play a part, the way we use our brain can make the difference in our response to the world and ultimately our health. This is the mind redefined.

Most of us don't spend a lot of time thinking about our brain or how to care for it unless we personally experience a problem. A strong family history of Alzheimer's Disease or other dementias, the impact of someone in our lives who had a stroke, or coping with the devastating results of a traumatic brain injury from a car accident or other trauma can all cause us to think about our brain and how to care for and protect it. We are responsible for keeping our brain in good working order. A balanced diet, appropriate supplements, and daily exercise all contribute to a healthy brain.

We can also teach our brain new skills. The same way that we learned to walk, play golf, or ride a bicycle, we can learn any skill if we are willing to put in the practice hours! Finally, we can actually create new pathways and connections in our brain by what we think about. The Bible calls this, "renewing your mind," (Romans 12:2). Science calls it neuroplasticity.

Modern science has shown that maintaining intellectual curiosity and staying socially active with others maintains brain health well into old age. Estrogen and oxytocin, two hormones found abundantly in the brain, significantly impact our ability to create protective social networks and initiate nurturing behaviors. In addition to hormones, our thoughts, attitudes, and emotions play a critical role in overall health.

This book contains many practical suggestions for achieving physical, emotional, and spiritual health and wellness. As founder of Oceanic Health Resources, Janet Leathem ARNP is a board-certified Psychiatric Nurse Practitioner and Clinical Nurse Specialist with a Biblical world view. Her passion is working with women to help them discover how God's unique design of the female brain, hormonal changes, and lifestyle choices impact a woman's emotional health. She has over 35 years of experience as a clinician, administrator, educator, and public speaker with a master's degree from Columbia University in NYC and a post-master's certificate as a Nurse Practitioner in Adult Mental Health from The Sage Colleges in Troy, NY. Her specialty is women's mental health & reproductive psychiatry. As the creator of The HEALTH Factor, a comprehensive plan for promoting wellness, her desire is to educate women of all ages to make choices that will help them reach optimal health by incorporating spiritual, emotional, and physical strategies.

However, this book is not intended to provide individual medical advice, diagnosis or treatment. All the content is for informational purposes only. Always seek personal advice from a qualified healthcare provider for questions about a medical condition. Never put off seeking advice because of something you read. I challenge you to *redefine your mind* and bring it into spiritual alignment with Biblical principles to promote peak health and wellness.

PREFACE

Modern brain science demonstrates that thoughts have a major impact on physical health. Current research shows that about 80% of physical illnesses can be caused by negative thinking. From a biochemical perspective, thoughts are simply electrical impulses, chemicals, and neurons, but they can have a profound impact on our bodies. Our thoughts can result in physical reactions, chemical imbalances, and inflammation—which lead to serious problems such as heart disease, diabetes, high blood pressure, depression, and arthritis.

God has given us a very intricate system of internal communication through our neurons. These neurons look like branches on a tree reaching out to another tree. Their connections can be strengthened or diminished based on our thoughts. Everyone has about 100 billion neurons and each one has 50,000 connections! As we process information, about 400 billion actions per second are taking place! Just the emotion of fear triggers more than 1,400 known physical and chemical responses. These responses activate more than 30 different hormones and neurotransmitters, throwing the body into a fight-or-flight state, preparing us to react to potential danger!

When our bodies are in this state of fight-or-flight, functions not needed for survival (such as our digestive system) are slowed or shut down and other functions that might help us survive (such as eyesight) are sharpened. Our heart rate increases as well as blood flow to muscles so we can run faster. Our body also increases the flow of hormones to an area of the brain known as the amygdala to help us focus on the presenting danger and store it in our memory. Once the fear pathways are ramped up, the brain short-circuits more rational processing paths and reacts immediately to signals from the amygdala or fear and anger center of the brain. When the brain is in this overactive state, it not only perceives events as negative, it remembers them that way! In fact, the world looks scary which is confirmed by memories stored in the hippocampus. The result is a person who feels anxious most of the time. Living under constant threat, whether perceived or actual, weakens our immune system and can cause damage to our heart and blood vessels, promote digestive problems such as ulcers and irritable bowel syndrome, and even decrease fertility. Can you see why our thoughts have a direct impact on our physical health?

Epigenetics is a new science that studies changes in organisms caused by the modification of gene expression. **The genetic code itself is not altered but specific genes can be turned "on" or "off" by stress, environment, and even thought patterns.** Mounting evidence has shown that children who are raised in a family environment with conflict, chaos, and lack of warmth develop a pro-inflammatory phenotype making them more susceptible to chronic diseases later in life. The Bible expressed this concept of epigenetics 3,000 years ago in Proverbs 23:7, *"As he thinks in his heart, so is he."*

Toxic thoughts are thoughts that trigger negative and anxious emotions. Examples include fear, anger, lack of forgiveness, and jealousy. The reason toxic thoughts are so dangerous to our health is that they produce biochemicals which cause the body stress. These biochemicals are stored not only in our minds but in the cells of our body as well. Ongoing scientific research continues to show us that the combination of our thoughts, emotions, and ultimately our attitudes can profoundly impact our bodies in either a positive or negative way. That change begins with our brains.

Over the last 20 years, brain science has been revolutionized by the discovery of neuroplasticity. Neuroplasticity is the brain's ability to reorganize itself by forming new connections between the neurons in our brains. Scientists have now shown that we can actually re-grow brain cells and change the structure and function of our brains by the way we think! The most interesting connections are between the thinking part of the brain called the prefrontal cortex (PFC) and the feeling part of the brain known as the limbic system. **The Bible calls this process of changing the structure and function of our brain by the way we think, "renewing our mind" (Romans 12:2).** It is thinking about our thoughts in a different way. Every time a thought enters our mind, we can either choose to strengthen or change it. By consciously becoming aware of our thought lives, we are re-transcribing and changing our neuronal networks and ultimately our brains. We cannot change our circumstances, *but* we can control our reactions to those circumstances and ultimately our health.

When we trust the Lord Jesus Christ as our Savior, the seeds of the fruit of the Holy Spirit are planted within our lives. These fruits are listed in

Galatians 5:22-23: *"But the fruit of the Spirit is love, joy, peace, longsuffering, kindness, goodness, faithfulness, gentleness, self-control."* Just like in a garden, those seeds need cultivation, including fertilizing, watering, pruning, and even weed-killer to encourage healthy growth. The characteristics and attitudes necessary to renew our mind and develop godly character include: forgiveness, thankfulness, confession of sin, obedience, and living in the wisdom of Christ.

Emotional health is the key to managing physical and spiritual health. Our thoughts have a profound impact on our overall well-being. Part I of this book discusses cutting edge neurological research as well as nutritional science to restart our body, renew our mind, and revive our spirit. As someone living in the 21st century with multiple priorities and demands including the continual electronic bombardment of cell phones, texts, and emails, brain strain has a tremendous impact on emotional health. Brain strain leads to the three "Ds" of *disappointment*, *discouragement*, and *depression*. Discover four important ways to control brain strain and reach optimal health. Science and scripture both claim that the spiritual foundation of health is based on the emotions of hope and happiness. The cultivation of happiness is one of the most important skills anyone can learn. Rewiring our brain for happiness, peace, and well-being is not only a spiritual exercise, it is based on the latest findings in neuroscience. By understanding our brains even a little bit, we can make a real difference in our well-being.

Part II of this book provides an opportunity to focus in a mindful way on the various fruits of the Spirit. Gardens are a prominent setting in the Scripture. It was in a garden that the man and the woman first encountered God, their Creator. Unfortunately, sin also began in the garden with the tree of the knowledge of good and evil. Thousands of years later it was in a garden that the Lord Jesus agonized in prayer with His Father in heaven about facing death on the cross as the payment for our sin, and it was in a garden that He was betrayed by one of His own disciples. Finally, it was in a garden that the empty tomb declared a risen Christ. God uses agriculture and fruit to teach us many lessons in Scripture including Cain's unacceptable offering of fruit from the sin-cursed ground, pomegranates on the hem of the high priest's garments speaking of fruitfulness for God, and vineyards illustrating our relationship with Christ and our need to abide in Him. The fruit of the Spirit is no exception.

Take at least 15 minutes every day to prayerfully and meditatively read the Bible verses and other inspirational sayings in each chapter that correspond to specific fruit of the Spirit. You will begin to renew your mind, root out toxic thoughts, and produce a harvest of fruit that will support optimal health. I would urge you to keep a journal of how you can specifically apply these thoughts to areas of your life that need fertilizing, watering, pruning, and weeding.

"Feed me with the food that is needful for me," (Proverbs 30:8 AMP). If you've ever planted a garden or even grown some potted plants, you know that fertilizer is to plants like food is to people. It contains all the nutrients and minerals that the plants need to grow healthy and strong. Without fertilizer the plants become weak, sickly, and may even die. Sometimes, plants which look limp and "half dead" will immediately spring back to life after a dose of Miracle Gro. The fertilizer is absorbed by the root system from the soil. We are like plants and need food too. If we feed on the written and the living Word of God - making time to meditate daily on Who Christ is, His amazing gift of salvation, and His plan for us - our lives will be like healthy, fruit bearing plants. The Apostle Paul instructed the early believers in Colosse to be "rooted and built up in Him and established in the faith . . . abounding in it with thanksgiving." Our root system needs to be nourished on the Word of God. If we are self-absorbed and disobedient, then our lives become unproductive and spiritually stunted. We must ask God to feed us with whatever is needful for us to serve Him in righteousness, in order that we grow in the knowledge of our Redeemer.

Water is an essential element in growing a garden. Seeds cannot germinate unless their hard outer shells are softened by the moist soil. So too, our hearts can become hardened without having communion with the Spirit of God. The Lord Jesus promised that when we receive the Holy Spirit, it would be like rivers of living water. Do you sometimes feel like you have a droopy spirit, or do you press on to know the Lord? Hosea 6:3 (NAS) instructs us to ". . .Let us press on to know the LORD. His going forth is as certain as the dawn; and He will come to us like the rain, like the spring rain watering the earth."

Pruning is important to maintain the health and fruit bearing ability of any plant or tree. Cutting away dead leaves or branches can cause a plant or tree to thrive. Dead leaves or branches can drain the plant of nutrients that could be going into new leaf growth or increasing the size and yield of the crop. God prunes away those things in our lives that have become old and useless. Sometimes that pruning is the removal of our "old ways" influenced by the world. Sometimes God prunes away our old concepts, and doctrines. Sometimes He allows us to suffer the loss of our health, or our ability to generate income, or touches other areas of our lives to learn dependence upon Him and grow healthier and stronger. Pruning will promote the fruit of the Spirit in our lives as we grow healthier and stronger. In John 15:1-2 Jesus says, "I am the true vine, and My Father is the vinedresser. Every branch in Me that does not bear fruit He takes away; and every branch that bears fruit He prunes, that it may bear more fruit."

The removal of weeds in the garden is useful because these unwanted plants compete with the crop for space, water and nutrients. Weeding can loosen the soil and allow water to reach the roots more easily. Almost immediately after a garden is planted, tiny weeds sprout right alongside the vegetable or flower seedlings. Both seedlings look almost identical when they first sprout making it difficult to tell the difference between the two. In the same way there are small weeds that grow in our hearts, and we are unaware of them until they become large enough to see. If God showed us all of the weak areas in our lives when they were too small to see, we would perhaps pluck up the good seed of what God is trying to do. He knows how and when to open our eyes to the weeds in the garden of our lives.

Weeds creep into our gardens in the same way that sin creeps into our lives, often when we are unaware of it. The Lord Jesus taught we must be careful to distinguish between the good seed and the weeds in the garden of our lives. Our standard for producing a good harvest comes from the Word of God which will allow us to distinguish between the "wheat and the tares." Only by spending time on a regular basis in the Scriptures will we be able to identify the tares (weeds) and purge them from the garden of our lives in order to produce the fruit of the Spirit.

God is concerned with the attitudes of our hearts. II Corinthians 10:5 tells us to *"bring every thought into captivity to the obedience of Christ."* Only then will our minds be renewed and our spirits restored!

To your continued good health,

Janet

THE BRAIN - THE CONTROL CENTER FOR EMOTIONS

MY STORY

Crippled following an elective surgery gone wrong, critically ill due to complications from infection, in excruciating chronic pain only partially relieved with opioid medication, nauseated and unable to eat, dependent on others for assistance with daily care, three heart attacks and five stents, an out-of-control thyroid with multiple symptoms, a cancer scare, forced disability retirement resulting in financial hardship and the need to sell our home, social isolation, role change, and the physical decline and death of both parents as well as an aunt who was like a second mother. . . Can you relate to any or perhaps all of these situations?

All of these events happened to me over five excruciating years and pummeled me like a jackhammer, grinding down the person I had become in the first 56 years of my life. I had reached the pinnacle of my career as a Nurse Executive running large nursing departments as well as obtaining board certification as a Psychiatric Nurse Practitioner. Stress upon stress, including the relentless demands and burdens of aging parents and young adult children, compounded any personal concerns. At my lowest point, the only thing that I could do was lie flat on my back and pray—when I wasn't in unmanageable pain or nauseated. Then, I couldn't even concentrate. My thoughts ran wild and my emotions were out of control. I remember my son, who was helping to care for me, say *"Mom, please stop moaning. . ."* Some very caring friends gave me their laptop so I could catch up with work from my hospital bed. Sadly, I wasn't even able to position myself to use it, let alone concentrate on anything due to the pain, nausea, and the darkness of an unknown future. It was only later that I discovered that my emotional self was the key to managing my physical and spiritual health.

As an evangelical Christian and a psychiatric nurse practitioner, I should have been in the best position to handle these crises. After all, I had helped many patients through the years with a variety of concerns. Depression, anxiety, pain management, addiction, bereavement, heart disease and other chronic illnesses, role changes, and financial concerns were no strangers to me. However, when they came knocking at my own door, I didn't know quite where to turn. Scriptures that were shared with me often left me feeling bewildered, helpless, and even hopeless as I began to believe that I had been abandoned by God. The world was dark and seemed to be closing in upon me even though I attempted to "put on a happy face" to those who visited and tried to give their support.

God's design for health incorporates physical, emotional, and spiritual dimensions. Regardless of our stage in life, we need to keep every dimension in balance. A young adult just beginning life's journey faces numerous stresses related to career choice, employment, marriage, and spiritual beliefs. A new mother adjusting to role changes and added responsibilities coupled with huge hormonal shifts also faces significant life stress. Even the "wisdom years" can bring suffering from bereavement over the loss of a loved one or "disenfranchised" grief due to retirement, financial loss, or social isolation and loneliness.

Stress has been shown to be a precursor to depression. Numerous studies have demonstrated how chronic depression is associated with increased cancer risk, increased risk of cardiac problems, increased mortality of hemodialysis patients, and an increase in inflammation demonstrated by elevated blood levels of inflammatory markers such as C-reactive protein and interlukin (IL) – 6. In addition, most researchers agree that there is a positive relationship between religious and spiritual practices and better health outcomes. Studies that compared spirituality to other health interventions including eating fruits and vegetables or taking blood pressure medicine found that people with a strong spiritual life had an 18% reduction in mortality. The evidence is overwhelming and continues to grow that balancing your body, mind, and spirit is essential to maximizing your health. Regardless of your circumstances, you can create your own toolbox of successful health strategies grounded in evidenced-based neuroscience as well as Biblical principles.

The **HEALTH Factor** is an acronym that I developed to help my patients effectively reach optimal health. Each letter represents an important pillar of support.

Hope & Happiness: The Spiritual Foundation for Health

Hope and happiness help us to see the big picture and bring meaning to our often chaotic lives. These two pursuits go together like a hand and glove. Simply pursuing happiness as an end in itself leads to a *taking* attitude, or giving the self what it wants. Hope on the other hand allows us to put aside our selfish interests and find meaning in Someone or something other than ourselves. The result is a *giving* attitude. According to researchers at Stanford University, people who have high meaning in their lives are more likely to help others in need. Our thinking, including our values, attitudes, and beliefs, actually change the structure of our brain, providing the spiritual foundation for health.

Exercise: The Energy for Health

The news is out: sitting is the new smoking. Sitting in an improper or slouched position for extended periods of time causes a physiologic change in the body. Prolonged sitting has been linked to an increased risk of diabetes, heart disease, and even early death. Muscle tissue can also degenerate, shrink, and weaken. According to the Mayo Clinic there are seven benefits of exercise—controlling weight, combating health conditions and diseases, improving mood, boosting energy, promoting better sleep, enhancing sex life, and just generally having fun! That is why exercise is considered the source of energy for reaching optimal health.

Amygdala/Brain Balance: The Relay Station for Health

The amygdala is the master center of emotions—particularly fear, anger, and aggression. It is an almond-shaped structure located deep in the temporal lobe of the brain and is part of the limbic system which contains structures related to emotions and physical drives such as thirst, appetite, sex, and sleep. The amygdala is responsible for processing memory and emotional reactions and as such serves as an amplifier or relay station for wellness. Counteracting brain strain and maintaining overall brain balance is essential to promoting our optimal health.

Lifestyle & Lab Values: The Sustainability of Health

Tracking lab values can provide an understanding of what's going on inside the body. Some of the important tests to check include Lipid Profile—a group of tests to determine risk of coronary heart disease, Complete Blood Count (CBC)—a broad screening to determine general health, Comprehensive Metabolic Panel (CMP)—to evaluate organ function and check for conditions such as diabetes, liver, and kidney disease, Thyroid Panel, and a baseline vitamin D level. Discuss these and other pertinent lab tests with your healthcare provider. Lifestyle includes diet, supplements, sleep patterns, social relationships, and finances, which all contribute to the sustainability of our health.

Toxic Thoughts: The Roadblock to Health

Toxic thoughts are the roadblock to health—and here's why. A toxic thought is any thought that generates negative emotions such as anger, anxiety, fear, or frustration. A review of modern scientific research over the past decade has demonstrated that *any* thought we have either positive or negative, is actively changing our body for better or for worse. The study of epigenetics has demonstrated that we can change which genes are activated in our bodies and ultimately change our health, as a direct result of our thought lives. This occurs because our thoughts activate or "tag" both good and bad genes. Therefore, what we think about has long-term consequences for our health! Toxic thoughts can activate genes that increase the risk for depression, heart disease, cancer, osteoporosis, and other chronic illnesses. That's why the writer of Proverbs tells us that "anxiety weighs down the heart. . ." (Proverbs 12:25 NIV). And the Psalmist says, "Cease from anger, and forsake wrath; Do not fret—it only causes harm," (Psalm 37:8).

Hormones: The Fuel for Health

Hormones supervise the function of every cell in our body. A woman's brain biochemistry is highly receptive to hormones and has countless receptor sites for the female sex hormones estrogen and progesterone. As hormone levels decline, the incidence of chronic, debilitating diseases such as arthritis, osteoporosis, mental decline, cancer, heart disease, obesity, loss of sex drive, incontinence, and many other problems increases. That's why hormones are considered the fuel for health. When the fuel level is low, chronic health problems increase.

The Merriam-Webster Dictionary defines factor as *"something that helps produce or influence a result: one of the things that causes something to happen."* When these principles are put into practice, the result is good physical, emotional and spiritual health regardless of the situation. Get acquainted with the various pillars of support for reaching optimal health, monitor your progress, and become your own health coach!

THE BRAIN AND YOUR EMOTIONS

Emotions exert an incredibly powerful force on our mood, behavior, and ultimately our health. They can make us feel like an out-of-control car going down the highway of life or as serene as a soft, billowy cloud floating through the sky, observing all of the chaos but not being impacted by it. We often make decisions based on whether we are happy, sad, frustrated, angry, or bored. Emotions can cause us to do something we might not normally do or avoid something that we generally enjoy doing.

Scientists have identified six basic emotions that are universal across all human cultures. These emotions are: disgust, anger, fear, surprise, happiness, and sadness. New research suggests that there may even only be four. People's facial expressions were observed and found that anger and disgust looked very similar, at least initially, as did fear and surprise. Anger and disgust shared a wrinkled nose and fear and surprise shared raised eyebrows. All emotions involve three components: a *subjective experience* or how you interpret a set of circumstances, a *physiological response* or how your body responds, and a *behavioral* or *expressive response.* The subjective experience of your emotions is influenced by your circumstances which often cause emotions to overlap. For example, a young woman preparing to get married can experience profound joy and overwhelming anxiety simultaneously.

Our brain is an amazing organ of the body. It is the command center that governs everything—not only our emotions, but our concrete and abstract thinking, memories, language and speech, breathing, heartbeat, blood pressure, coordination, balance, and posture. No two people have the same brain because none of us have the same experiences—not even twins. Our brains develop at different rates based on what we do and learn. Our neurons or nerve cells split and rewire based on our experiences. The brain determines our response to stress and even our ability to get a good night's sleep. There are nerves that register pleasure and pain as well as transmit perceptions, thoughts, feelings, and emotions. The brain does all of this by the means of chemical messengers called neurotransmitters. Some examples of neurotransmitters include: serotonin, norepinephrine, dopamine, and acetylcholine. Perhaps you are familiar with serotonin and its relation to depression. In fact, a whole class of antidepressants is labeled as selective serotonin reuptake inhibitors or SSRIs. Some SSRIs that may be familiar include Zoloft (sertraline), Prozac (fluvoxetine), Celexa (citalopram), and Lexapro (escitalopram).

The prefrontal-limbic system of your brain plays a major role in the processing of emotions, the regulation of moods, and the storage of memories. The pre-frontal cortex (located in the front of your brain) rules the emotions. It puts the brakes on the amygdala which is in the limbic system (located deep inside your brain) and keeps your emotions under control. One of my patients, whom I shall call Susan, was a relatively easy-going, 27-year-old woman. However, both she and her family noticed that in the last week of her menstrual cycle her mood became very irritable. Little things that normally wouldn't bother her became "issues." She often found herself yelling at her husband and children or crying for silly reasons. She tried to hide the emotions, but she finally came for treatment because she recognized that this emotional rollercoaster was dramatically interfering with both her home life and her work as a schoolteacher. What Susan was experiencing was a particular *sensitivity* to the *normal* cyclical premenstrual hormonal fluctuations which resulted in a chemical dysregulation in her brain. Her pre-frontal cortex was no longer able to inhibit or buffer angry and aggressive impulses. Willpower, self-discipline, and prayer could not manage her mood. It was a biological problem involving her brain and her hormones.

Monthly fluctuations of estrogen and progesterone cause a huge impact on both the serotonergic and dopaminergic mood pathways in your brain. GABA (gamma amnio-butyric acid), the main inhibitory neurotransmitter, may also play a role. Evidence continues to validate that serotonin in particular is implicated in PMS (Pre-Menstrual Syndrome) and PMDD (Premenstrual Dysphoric Disorder). Symptoms of irritability, depressed mood, and carbohydrate craving are thought to be associated with low levels of serotonin.

By self-monitoring her moods on a monthly mood chart, Susan was able to identify that her dramatic mood volatility coincided with the last week of her menstrual cycle. I also gave her additional tools to monitor her diet, exercise, and sleep patterns for two months. This information helped us to implement certain lifestyle modifications, nutritional supplementation, and medication and hormonal management changes which happily resulted in a positive outcome. While there is not solid evidence about certain lifestyle changes, cutting back on or eliminating caffeine, sugar, alcohol, and nicotine can be helpful. Ensuring that you get adequate sleep is essential as well. Read the chapter on "Use Your Brain to Overcome Insomnia" for some suggestions. Aerobic exercise has also been demonstrated to be effective in helping to alleviate both the physical and emotional symptoms of PMS and PMDD.

Certain nutritional supplements including calcium (1200 mg.), B6 (50 – 100 mg.), magnesium (200 – 360 mg.), and vitamin E (400 IU) have been shown to provide some modest relief of symptoms as well. In particular, a large multi-center study showed that taking calcium 1200 mg. daily decreased both physical and emotional symptoms. Another double-blind, placebo-controlled study showed that chasteberry (1 mg.) significantly decreased the premenstrual symptoms of irritability, anger, headaches, and breast fullness when compared to placebo. Another non-pharmacological treatment approach is Cognitive Behavioral Therapy or CBT. CBT has been demonstrated to be as effective as fluoxetine (Prozac) 20 mg. in treating PMDD. However, if an antidepressant is indicated, selective serotonin reuptake inhibitors (SSRIs) are the first choice. Numerous studies have shown that, in general, women respond to low doses of SSRIs, and the response usually only takes a few days.

An important factor that you need to consider before choosing to treat your symptoms with an antidepressant is whether or not you have an underlying mood disorder or another medical condition. Other medical conditions that have features overlapping with PMDD include: chronic fatigue syndrome, fibromyalgia, irritable bowel syndrome, and migraine disorder. These conditions should be adequately controlled before addressing PMDD symptoms. Also, about 40% of women who seek treatment for PMDD have an underlying mood disorder such as unipolar or bipolar depression with mood worsening during the premenstrual phase. This change in mood during the last two weeks of the menstrual cycle is known as Premenstrual Exacerbation (PME) and the symptoms can mimic PMDD.

Margaret, a 32-year-old, single woman with a diagnosis of Bipolar I Disorder was one of my patients while I worked on the inpatient behavioral health unit. She was a "frequent flyer" and kept reappearing for admission to the hospital on a fairly regular basis. No matter how we tried to tweak her treatment, she continued to routinely decompensate to the point of needing readmission to the hospital. Then at one of our treatment team meetings, someone suggested that perhaps Margaret had what is known as Premenstrual Exacerbation (PME) of her bipolar disorder. We taught Margaret how to track her symptoms and record them on a mood chart for two months. After reviewing her mood pattern, it became evident that Margaret was overly sensitive to hormonal fluctuations in the luteal phase (the last two weeks) of her menstrual cycle. Since she had no history of blood clots, strokes, or migraines, and was not a smoker, she was started on an oral contraceptive. The rationale was that by suppressing her ovulation, her premenstrual symptoms would be eliminated. Adding a birth control pill to Margaret's routine bipolar treatment helped to keep her symptoms under control and the frequency of her hospital admissions dramatically dropped.

NEUROPLASTICITY AND "RENEWING OUR MIND"

Neuroplasticity is the brain's ability to reorganize itself by forming new connections between neurons throughout our lives. The brain structure or its anatomy as well as its functional organization or physiology can actually change. We can influence that change by the way we think!

For many years neuroscientists believed that the brain was a static organ, meaning that it did not change after a certain point in our growth and development. It has only been in the last 20 years that scientists have shown that we actually can re-grow brain cells and change our brains throughout our lives. The brain is rewired, meaning that the connections between one region and another become stronger or different. This rewiring is particularly important when it affects the connections between the thinking part of the brain (the prefrontal cortex) and the feeling part of the brain (the limbic system). When you think about a situation in a different way, these neuronal connections actually change by either strengthening or weakening.

A neuron or nerve cell has 3 parts to it:

- **A cell body**: containing a nucleus with DNA, endoplasmic reticulum, mitochondria and other organelles.
- **The dendrites:** bringing information to the cell body. The dendrites resemble small tree branches, allowing the neuron to connect to multiple neurons. They allow the neuron to talk to other cells or perceive the environment, and are the place where memories are stored.
- **The axon:** bringing information away from the cell body to the connecting neuron. It is the longest fiber of the neuron.

Dendrites grow extensively on the nerve cell as we think. Conversely, the dendrites or branches can shrink or fall off with continued high levels of stress. As we change our thinking, some branches go away and new ones form. The strength of the connections also change and the memories network with other thoughts. The Bible calls this *"renewing your mind"* (Romans 12:2). Our mind and body are inherently linked by our thoughts. Every time we think a thought and it dominates our conscious mind, protein synthesis happens. We can do something with that thought. We can either choose to strengthen the thought or change it by laying down new circuits. By consciously becoming aware of our thought lives, we are re-transcribing and changing our neuronal networks.

Cognitive Behavioral Therapy or CBT is a very powerful form of therapy to help a person become aware of cognitive distortions or habitual negative thoughts. These faulty thought patterns can lead us to spiral into depression which can ultimately lead to serious health consequences. What occurs is that our thoughts influence our emotions which in turn can influence your behavior. Dr. Aaron Beck, MD, the founder of CBT, defined this internal talk as *automatic thoughts* that occur in response to whatever situation you may be facing at a particular time.

Here's an example from one of my patients. Cindy was having a bad day at work. She had multiple deadlines to meet in order to complete an important project and the day's interruptions were endless. When a coworker offered her some support, she didn't even notice because she was so focused on everything that was going wrong. She couldn't wait until the end of the day. When quitting time arrived, she was relieved to get into her car to start the commute home. But in just a few minutes, she was caught up in a huge traffic jam on the highway. As she attempted to merge onto the highway, a kind man waved her on so that she could merge safely. However, just a few minutes later, another driver cut her off while changing lanes. She told me that her reaction to her commute home was to grumble to herself that there are only rude and insensitive people in her city! This type of cognitive distortion is called a mental filter. Although the first driver had courteously let her into the flow of traffic, she totally disregarded his consideration when the second driver cut her off. Her mental filter caused her to only focus on the negative experience rather than the positive one. You can find a more detailed discussion about cognitive distortions in the chapter on "Brain Strain." There you can discover the 10 basic cognitive distortions and which ones may apply to you.

We cannot change our circumstances BUT we can control our reactions to those circumstances. The Contemporary English Version of Romans 12:2 puts it this way, "Let God change the way you think. . ."

As we have already emphasized, thoughts are not harmless. Toxic thoughts which trigger negative emotions such as fear, anger, lack of forgiveness, hatred, and frustration, produce biochemicals that cause the body stress. Toxic thinking can become dangerous to you physically, emotionally, or spiritually because these thoughts are not only stored in your mind but in the cells of your body as well. Dr. Caroline Leaf, a researcher in the science of thought, says that "toxic thoughts are like poison or an abscess to the brain."

Thoughts are scientifically measurable and scientists can actually verify their effect on our bodies and our emotions. Stressful times can frequently result in a person becoming ill such as catching a cold or having an arthritis flare-up. Digestion problems including constipation or diarrhea can also become a problem for some. These illnesses were probably not a coincidence but rather the direct result of inflammation and a stressed immune system, with toxic thoughts as the starting point. Every thought that we have creates a corresponding emotion and that emotion is linked to a memory which is stored in our brain and our body's cells.

That is why we are instructed in II Corinthians 10:3-5 to "*bring every thought into captivity to the obedience of Christ.*" Positive thoughts strengthen positive reaction chains and release biochemicals into our bodies such as endorphins (which block pain sensation), dopamine (which controls the reward and pleasure centers), and serotonin (which contributes to feelings of well-being and happiness). So once again you can see how spiritual health is intertwined with both physical and emotional health.

Neurogenesis, literally the birth of neurons, is the process by which new neurons are generated. Neurogenesis occurs in the hippocampus and the cerebellum, as well as other parts of the brain. It is important to note that the hippocampus is larger and more active in women. Studies have shown that adult neurogenesis is important for learning and memory. It plays an important role in healthy aging. According to the Society for Neuroscience, excessive stress has been shown to "alter brain cells, brain structure and brain function." Chronic stress, depression, and sleep deprivation negatively impact the birth of new nerve cells. On the other hand, exercise has been shown to increase the formation of new neurons, and which again demonstrates the benefits of physical activity on the brain. That is why the HEALTH Factor identifies exercise as the energy for health.

Dr. Shephard Kantor, a noted psychiatrist and researcher at the Columbia University College of Physicians and Surgeons, has hypothesized that emotional wounds at any point throughout life, can create the alterations in the brain that cause mood disorders. He suggested that the mood changes produced by depression may be due to certain sensations and memory traces that go back to childhood. Events from that time, he theorizes, produce changes in the neurotransmitter levels or receptor sites of the brain. The capacity for emotions such as joy, happiness, fear, and shyness are already developed at birth. The Bible gives much instruction related to godly parenting and appropriate emotional expression. Family, community, and religious and cultural expectations all help to regulate the development and expression of our emotions. Our epigenome tags physically mark our DNA in a way that affects how our genes operate. Developing research continues to demonstrate that close, secure, interpersonal relationships promote a safe environment to explore, learn, and therefore promote a *developing capacity* for mental health. We have an awesome responsibility as Christian parents to help shape our children's emotional health.

The apostle Paul knew what he was talking about when he says in Philippians 4:8, "Finally, brethren, whatever things are true, whatever things are noble, whatever things are just, whatever things are pure, whatever things are lovely, whatever things are of good report, if there is any virtue and if there is anything praiseworthy—meditate (reflect on or contemplate) on these things." Don't let toxic thoughts be the roadblock to your emotional health!

BRAIN HEMISPHERES

A deep furrow separates the brain into the left and right hemispheres. Both sides are connected by a bundle of nerve fibers known as the corpus callosum or the "caring membrane." In recent years, there has been some controversy over the notion that each hemisphere has unique functions and works independently. While it is true that some brain functions occur more in one side than the other, recent research has shown that people don't tend to have a stronger left- or right-sided brain network. The pop-psychology idea of dominant left brain/right brain thinking has been debunked. According to this theory, the right side of the brain is best at expressive and creative tasks such as recognizing faces, reading and expressing emotions, music, color, and creativity. The left side of the brain is skilled at tasks involving logic, language, and analytical thinking. Neuroscientists now know, however, that both sides of the brain work together to perform a variety of tasks. For example, language tends to be on the left or logic side of the brain, and attention more on the right or intuitive and creative side. However, the left hemisphere specializes in picking out the sounds that form words and figuring out the arrangement of words in a sentence. The right hemisphere is more sensitive to the emotional features of the language, such as the rhythm or tone. In general, both sides of the brain were shown to be essentially equal in their activity according to a large study of 1000 participants at the University of Utah.

Both sides of the brain are involved with mood states as well. The right side tends to be responsible for negative, unhappy emotions. The left side focuses on positive, even euphoric feelings. If both sides are working together, your mood is balanced. When the right side of the brain is damaged and the left side dominates, a person's mood becomes inappropriately happy. An injury to the left side of the brain leads to depression because the right side dominates. It is important to become familiar with some of the key structures of the brain in order to understand how biochemical changes can affect your mood, behavior, and ultimately, your health.

SEVEN EMOTIONAL COMPONENTS OF THE BRAIN: THE PREFRONTAL-LIMBIC COMPLEX

"We create words to define our experience and those words bring attendant emotions that jerk us around like dogs on a leash."
–Elizabeth Gilbert

Do you sometimes feel jerked around by your emotions? What words are you playing in your head that define who you are and influence your emotions and behavior? *I'm a failure. I'm lonely. I'm disorganized. I'm anxious. I'm frustrated. I can't cope. I'm angry. I'm stupid.* Or perhaps your words are more positive—*I'm confident. I'm successful. I'm popular. I'm happy. I'm likeable.* Your thoughts define your emotions and your emotions shape your personality and behavior. But where do these emotions originate?

There are seven key areas of the brain that particularly impact emotions and behaviors. These areas are part of what is often referred to as **the prefrontal-limbic complex** and play a large role in the processing of emotions, the regulation of moods, and the storage of memories. The prefrontal cortex is located in the front of the brain and the limbic system is located deep within the brain. The "junction box" linking the prefrontal cortex and the limbic area is found in a part of the brain known as Area 25. This area is extremely rich in serotonin transporters and was found to be over-active in people who have treatment resistant depression - their depressive symptoms are difficult to control or reach remission. According to Dr. Helen Mayberg, a board certified neurologist, this area is like a "gate left open" in people who do not respond to depression treatment—

allowing negative emotions to overwhelm thinking and mood. When this area was stimulated with electrodes using a procedure known as deep brain stimulation, there was a 60% response rate after six months that was maintained long-term with continued stimulation.

1 PREFRONTAL CORTEX: THE CONTROL CENTER FOR EMOTIONS

The prefrontal cortex or PFC is in the very front of the brain, right behind the forehead. It takes up over a third of the brain's volume and is responsible for keeping your emotions under control. The prefrontal cortex is larger in women and matures faster in teen girls than in boys by one to two years. It is the area of the brain responsible for higher-level thinking, such as making decisions and solving problems. It helps you pay attention, be organized, and solve tricky problems. Different parts of the PFC are involved in using short-term or "working" memory and in retrieving long-term memories. This area of the brain also helps control the amygdala during stressful events. The amygdala is found in the limbic area of the brain and is responsible for fear, anger, and aggression.

When the prefrontal cortex is damaged physically or chemically, judgment is impaired, emotions become shallow and blunted, and motivation and drive disappear. People become irritable and easily enraged, and their moods can become depressed or apathetic.

John, a 47-year-old, white male, was a well-adjusted, mild-mannered, professional accountant with no psychiatric history. He was married for 10 years to his wife Molly, and they had two adult children. One Saturday, he was doing some chores around the house which included cleaning leaves out of the roof gutters. That was when his entire life completely changed! John fell off the ladder and suffered a traumatic brain injury which affected his prefrontal cortex. I met John during his second hospitalization following the accident. According to Molly, his entire personality and behavior completely changed. A psychiatric consultation was ordered because he became violent and verbally abusive with threatening behaviors. The injury to his prefrontal cortex dramatically changed his personality and behavior, and he was no longer able to buffer the angry and aggressive impulses coming through from the amygdala in the limbic area of his brain. Medications helped a bit, but he often ended up needing to be restrained to control his behaviors. Both his children and his wife were devastated by the change in his behavior.

Some research shows that people who have either post-traumatic stress disorder (PTSD) or attention deficit hyperactivity disorder (ADHD) have reduced activity in their PFCs. Another example of prefrontal dysregulation occurs with premenstrual dysphoric disorder (PMDD), which causes a woman to experience rage, anger, irritability, and hostility. The chemical dysregulation in the brain extends from the limbic system into the cortex. Premenstrual hormonal fluctuations can interfere with the PFC's ability to inhibit or buffer angry and aggressive impulses. For women who are sensitive to hormonal fluctuations, the premenstrual period can become a living nightmare!

The power of choice is located in the brain's frontal lobe. Judgment, reasoning, social norms, and long-term planning all take place in this decision center of our brain. The ability to choose is a powerful asset given to us by our Creator. None of us can change our yesterdays, but we can all actively live in the present moment, and by making wise choices, change our tomorrows. Deuteronomy 30:19 gives us the instructions, "Choose life." The book of James teaches, "If any of you lacks wisdom, let him ask of God, who gives to all liberally and without reproach, and it will be given to him. But let him ask in faith, with no doubting, for he who doubts is like a wave of the sea driven and tossed by the wind." Do you sometimes feel like a wave, being tossed about by the circumstances of your life? Spiritual, emotional, and physical health are all inter-related and the choices you make will determine if you stay on course. You are only one choice away from improving your health!

In the Gospel of Mark we read a story about a paralytic who was carried by four men to Jesus. The house in Capernaum where Jesus was preaching was so crowded that they couldn't even get near the Lord. However, that didn't stop them. They made a choice that only the Lord could heal their friend and they acted in faith. Circumstances did not stop them! Even though they couldn't get near the door, they broke through the roof and let down the bed on which the paralyzed man was lying. He landed right in front of the Savior. However, an unexpected thing happened. Instead of immediately healing him physically, Jesus saw their faith and said to the paralytic, "Son, your sins are forgiven you," (Mark 2:5). The paralyzed man and his four friends could have responded like the scribes who reasoned within themselves, "Why does this Man speak blasphemies like this? Who can forgive sins but God alone?" (Mark 2:6). However, they accepted Christ's forgiveness by faith. Spiritual healing is essential for complete and total wellness. Jesus then responded, "'That you may know that the Son of Man has power on earth to forgive sins. . .I say to you, arise, take up your bed, and go to your house.' Immediately, he arose, took up the bed, and went out in the presence of them all. . ." (Mark 2:10-12).

#2 ANTERIOR CINGULATE CORTEX: MOTIVATION, FOCUS, AND THE "WORRY-WORT CENTER"

Another important structure that affects your emotions and behaviors is called the Anterior Cingulate Cortex or ACC. It is located near the top of the frontal lobes and along the walls that divide the left and right hemispheres. The ACC has many different roles, from controlling blood pressure and heart rate to responding when we sense a mistake, to helping us feel motivated and stay focused on a task, and managing proper emotional reactions. Reduced ACC activity or damage to this brain area has been linked to disorders such as attention deficit hyperactivity disorder (ADHD), schizophrenia, and depression.

The ACC functions as an early warning system. It warns us in advance when our behavior might lead to a negative outcome, so that we can be more careful and avoid making a mistake. It does this by monitoring environmental cues, weighing possible consequences and options, and adjusting behavior to avoid danger. It's what kicks into gear when you walk into a crowded room of strangers during a business meeting or social function. You may find yourself scanning the crowd to find "safe" people with whom to interact, who will not prove to be too challenging. The Anterior Cingulate Cortex is larger in women than in men and is sometimes referred to as the "worry-wort" center. It influences our fight or flight reaction when we face danger. It is also thought to be involved with postpartum obsessive compulsive disorder or OCD. Hormonal influences coupled with a heightened activity in the Anterior Cingulate Cortex may be responsible for the dread and anxiety that some women experience when they are unable to fulfill their obsessions about harming their baby.

Hormonal changes during the postpartum period can cause the brain to dysregulate, especially in women who are more sensitive to hormonal fluctuations. Estrogen and progesterone are highest at the end of pregnancy. As soon as the placenta is delivered, the hormone levels drop precipitously. In fact, estrogen levels reach that of a normal menstrual cycle within 24 hours! In addition, there are vast numbers of estrogen receptors in the limbic brain, the part of the brain responsible for our emotions. If estrogen contributes to mood stability, imagine how profoundly its rapid removal can impair mood health in vulnerable women. Serotonin pathways are the pathways primarily involved in OCD symptoms and estrogen has a major effect within the serotonin pathways.

Michele was a 26-year-old, first-time mother about three weeks postpartum. She had an uneventful pregnancy and delivery with no history of psychiatric problems. One afternoon she appeared at my office door clutching her baby. She was visibly shaken. I had seen her during her postpartum stay in the hospital so she knew where to turn for help. When she calmed down enough to talk, she told me that she was having scary thoughts about harming her baby. Several days previously, while making dinner, she thought about what would happen if she put her baby in the microwave. Too frightened to even discuss her thoughts with her husband, she kept them to herself. Then today, while driving up to her house with the baby in the car, she saw her husband clipping the hedges. She thought to herself, *I wonder what would happen if I put the baby's arm in the hedge clippers?* She also had a recurrent image of the baby dying either from being dropped or from choking. Michele was totally aware of her thoughts, coherent, and not delusional. She was having scary obsessions related to harm befalling her newborn infant either accidentally or intentionally, but in no way perceived her thoughts to harm the baby as a "good idea" which would indicate postpartum psychosis. After a brief hospitalization and some outpatient Interpersonal Therapy, Michele was on the road to recovery.

#3 INSULA: THE MIND/ BODY CONNECTION

The insula is a prune-size structure deep within the brain which processes gut feelings. It also is larger and more active in women. According to Dr. Martin Paulus, a psychiatrist at the University of California, San Diego, and others, the mind and body are integrated in the insula. It is a sort of receiving zone that reads the physiological state of the entire body, including cravings and hunger states, and then generates subjective feelings that can bring about actions—like reaching for that yummy dessert, smoking another cigarette, having another glass of wine, or abusing pain medication. It strives to keep the body in a state of internal balance. Current research on the insula is being used to discover new ways to treat drug addiction, alcoholism, anxiety, and eating disorders.

There are actually two insula, one on each side of the brain which are part of multiple circuits. Information from the insula is relayed to other brain structures that appear to be involved in decision making, especially the anterior cingulate cortex and the prefrontal cortex.

Arthur D. Craig at the Barrow Neurological Institute in Phoenix described the circuitry that connects the body to the insula. In humans, information about the body's state is picked up in the brain from signals coming from the gut, the heart, the lungs, and other internal organs. We all have experienced this feeling at one time or another. We're in an unfamiliar situation or perhaps we come face-to-face with someone or something uncomfortable. Our heart starts pounding, we begin breathing faster, and perhaps we feel a knot in our stomach. We also become more acutely aware of our surroundings.

The insula also recasts sensations as social emotions. For example, a bad taste or smell may be sensed in the frontal insula as disgust. The frontal insula is where people sense love and hate, gratitude and resentment, self-confidence and embarrassment, trust and distrust, empathy and contempt, approval and disdain, pride and humiliation, truthfulness and deception, atonement and guilt. People who are better at reading these sensations score higher on psychological tests of empathy. And just as a reminder: the insula is larger and more active in women.

THE LIMBIC SYSTEM: CONTROLS BASIC DRIVES AND EMOTIONS INCLUDING PAIN, ANGER, HUNGER, SEX, THIRST, TEMPERATURE, AND PLEASURE

The limbic system includes four major areas of the brain: the hypothalamus, amygdala, pituitary gland, and hippocampus. All the functions that sustain and protect life such as appetite, thirst, sleep-wake cycle, sex drive, aggressive impulses, memory, body temperature, and control of the menstrual cycle are regulated by the structures in the limbic brain. However, the limbic brain does not give us the ability to think, use language, or understand complex abstract processes. That occurs in the prefrontal cortex. If an object or event is perceived as a danger, the limbic brain must decide within milliseconds whether it represents a real threat. If the brain is not sure, a biochemical response occurs which may lead to a sense of being hyper-alert and on guard—often referred to as the stress response. What happens is that a cascade of biochemical changes mobilizes the secretion of a series of stress hormones that activate your body to respond in one of three ways: flee, fight, or freeze with fear.

An essential but often unacknowledged component of women's mental health is the fact that estrogen and progesterone significantly influence all of the neurochemical pathways involved in mood disturbances, and these hormonal receptors are most dense in the limbic area. Estrogen, in particular, maintains the orderly firing rates of the serotonin, dopamine, acetylcholine, and norepinephrine nerve cells. So the limbic system is an essential component to understanding our moods.

#4 HYPOTHALAMUS: RELAY STATION OF EMOTIONS

The hypothalamus is the control center of the body's organs. It functions as a switching station translating instructions from the brain carried by neurochemical signals into hormonal signals that travel through the bloodstream. It coordinates your heart rate, blood pressure, and respirations as well as stimulates your hormones by secreting special hormones known as releasing factors. The hypothalamus orchestrates the menstrual cycle, thyroid function, the stress response, body temperature, sleep-wake cycle, appetite, growth, and milk production. It is an extremely powerful part of the brain which links the nervous system to the endocrine system via the pituitary gland. Once the pituitary gland becomes activated during puberty, the "chemical brakes" are taken off the hypothalamus and, in women, something called the hypothalamic-pituitary-ovarian system begins to function. It serves as the first relay system of emotions from the amygdala to the rest of the body.

As estrogen and progesterone begin to surge during puberty, female specific brain circuits become more sensitive to emotional interactions such as approval and disapproval or acceptance and rejection. The filter through which a woman interprets feedback from others becomes heightened. She can hear a wider spectrum of emotional tone. During perimenopause as the brain begins to experience estrogen withdrawal, one symptom that may develop is hot flashes. The hypothalamus responds to the estrogen decrease by changing its heat-regulating cells, resulting in a woman suddenly feeling tremendously hot even in normal temperatures.

Another function of the hypothalamus is to jump start the sexual organs into gear. Testosterone is the chemical fuel that gets the brain's sexual engine going. It revs the hypothalamus, igniting erotic feelings, sexual fantasies, and physical sensations. Sex-related centers in the male brain are two times larger than the female brain. In fact, you might say that men have the equivalent of the Miami International Airport as a hub for processing thoughts about sex while women have the local Fort Lauderdale Executive Airport. On the other hand, women have an eight-lane superhighway for processing emotions while men have only a country road! But I'm sure you already know this. . .

#5 AMYGDALA: MASTER CENTER FOR ANGER, FEAR, AND AGGRESSION

The amygdala is the master center for anger, fear, and aggression. Louann Brizendine MD, a neuropsychiatrist at the University of California, San Francisco, called the amygdala "the wild beast within." It is primarily held in check by the prefrontal cortex which is the brain's control center. Studies have shown that both men and women report feeling the same amount of anger, however, the expression of anger and aggression is greater in men. The reason is that the amygdala is physically larger in men. It contains many testosterone receptors which stimulate and heighten his response to anger, making it easier to push a man's anger button. This is why some men can escalate within seconds to a fist fight.

On the other hand, when women are confronted with fear, loss, or pain, the PFC and the anterior cingulate cortex, which are the thinking parts of the brain, are quickly called into action. It's the brain's version of the "extra stomach" for chewing on anger. However, language and speech are located in the PFC, so when a woman's faster verbal circuits kick into gear, they can unleash a barrage of angry words that a man can't match. Changing hormonal conditions during the menstrual cycle also add volatility to the amygdala causing irritability and mood swings. Many young teenage girls are particularly sensitive to shifts in hormones in this area of the brain resulting in emotional outbursts and impulsive behavior.

When stress or fear triggers the amygdala, anxiety may result. The brain focuses all its conscious attention on the threat at hand. Anxiety is four times more common in women than in men. This is due to the fact that a woman has a highly responsive stress trigger, allowing her to become anxious much more quickly than a man.

The amygdala also appears to be involved in learning to fear an event, such as touching a hot stove, as well as learning not to fear, such as overcoming a fear of heights. Researchers are studying how the amygdala helps create memories of fear and safety to help find improved treatments for anxiety disorders like phobias or post-traumatic stress disorder (PTSD).

#6 PITUITARY: THE MASTER GLAND OF THE BODY CONTROLLING MILK PRODUCTION, GROWTH, SEX HORMONES, THYROID, STRESS, INTIMACY, AND WATER BALANCE

Another organ in the limbic system is the pituitary gland. The pituitary has a profound impact on your emotions because of its role in producing and stimulating hormones throughout the body. It is a tiny gland, about the size of a pea, found at the base of the brain and is the master gland of the body. The pituitary consists of two parts: the anterior and posterior pituitary.

Hormones secreted by the anterior or front portion of the pituitary influence growth, sexual development, skin pigmentation, thyroid function, and adrenal function. The pituitary gland makes eight types of hormones:

• *Prolactin* which stimulates milk production after childbirth to enable nursing and also affects sex hormone levels from ovaries in women and from testes in men.

• *Growth hormone (GH)* which stimulates growth in childhood and is important for maintaining muscle mass, bone mass, and fat distribution in the body.

• *Adrenocorticotropin (ACTH)* which stimulates the production of cortisol, the "stress hormone," by the adrenal glands. It also helps to maintain blood pressure and blood glucose levels.

• *Thyroid-stimulating hormone (TSH)* which stimulates the thyroid gland, the regulator of the body's metabolism, energy, growth, and nervous system activity.

• *Luteinizing hormone (LH)* which regulates testosterone in men and estrogen in women.

• *Follicle-stimulating hormone (FSH)* which promotes sperm production in men and stimulates the ovaries to enable ovulation in women. Luteinizing hormone and follicle-stimulating hormone work together to cause normal function of the ovaries and testes.

The posterior pituitary, or the back portion of the pituitary, secretes the hormones oxytocin and antidiuretic hormone.

• *Oxytocin* is the hormone of intimacy. It also increases uterine contractions. An experiment on hugging, revealed that oxytocin is naturally released in the brain after a twenty-second hug from a partner—sealing the bond and triggering the brain's trust circuits. Touching, gazing, positive social interaction, kissing, and sexual orgasm all release oxytocin in the female brain.

• *Antidiuretic hormone (ADH)* is also called vasopressin. It regulates water balance by increasing reabsorption of water by the kidneys.

So the take home message about the pituitary is that it produces hormones of fertility, milk production, and nurturing behavior, and therefore is the key which turns on the "mommy brain." The pituitary also stimulates the adrenal glands in both men and women to produce cortisol, and therefore, influences the stress reaction. It is essential that these hormones remain in balance in order to maintain optimal health.

For example, TSH levels are important to be monitored and are one of the lab values that your healthcare provider should be checking annually. The HEALTH Factor calls "L" Lifestyle and Lab Values: The Sustainability of Health. Thyroid and mood problems affect about 40 million Americans. The prevalence of hyperthyroidism, or over-active thyroid, is around five per 1000 and hypothyroidism about three per 1000 women. The American Association of Clinical Endocrinologists is recommending that the normal range for TSH run from 0.3 mIU/L to 3.0 mIU/L. When TSH is elevated it indicates that your thyroid is underactive or that you have hypothyroidism. Hypothyroidism can present with the following symptoms: mild to severe fatigue, depression, unexplained weight gain, heavier than normal menstrual cycles, and cognitive and memory problems. Many run-of-the-mill depression diagnoses actually have thyroid as the underlying cause. In fact, published journal studies suggest that the figure is as high as 30-40%. If a person has a thyroid and mood problem and is given an antidepressant like Prozac (fluvoxatine) or Zoloft (sertraline), they will experience little to no benefit but in fact may experience substantial side effects.

This was the case with Lillian. Her primary care provider was treating her for symptoms of depression including fatigue, increased weight, depressed mood, and insomnia. When she did not improve on Zoloft 50 mg. after about two months, she was referred to psychiatry for follow-up. I saw her as an outpatient and obtained a comprehensive history. When I realized that her thyroid levels had not been checked, I ordered a thyroid panel to check not only her TSH but also her free T4. She was diagnosed with hypothyroidism and started on Synthroid 75 mcg. daily. Within six months, Lillian was stabilized on her thyroid medication and was able to be discontinued from her Zoloft. Her mood improved and she was sleeping better.

#7 HIPPOCAMPUS: THE MEMORY STORAGE COMPARTMENT

The seventh area of the brain impacting emotions and mood is the hippocampus, the memory storage compartment of the brain. The hippocampus is a paired structure located in both the left and right brain hemispheres and is shaped like a horseshoe. It is involved in memory forming by organizing and storing information. It connects emotions which are generated from thoughts and senses, such as smell and sound, to memories. It helps to create and file new memories. A sight or a sound can generate an emotion, either good or bad, which is registered as a memory in the hippocampus. The hippocampus may be involved in mood disorders through its control of a major mood circuit called the hypothalamic-pituitary-adrenal (HPA) axis.

The hippocampus is larger in women. You may have observed that women have a better memory for the details of both pleasant and unpleasant emotional experiences. A woman can recall a detailed three-dimensional sensory snapshot, i.e. when the event happened, who was there, what the weather was like, how the restaurant smelled, what people were wearing, etc. The stronger the amygdala (the fear, anger, and aggression center in the limbic system) responds to a stressful situation and the thoughts that are generated, the more details that the hippocampus will tag for memory storage about the experience. There is one exception with men. If a man has an angry or threatening interaction, he will register the emotion with detailed memories as quickly as a woman can. So for example if a woman threatens her partner verbally or physically, it will get his attention, and he will vividly remember the argument.

Powerful recollections from childhood are fixed in the pre-frontal limbic complex. These thoughts can shape a person's development and their adult life by laying down memories and the emotions attached to them—pleasant or unpleasant. Smells and sounds can trigger memories as well as emotions. These memories are sometimes fragmented because the experiences are recorded in the limbic system in a fragmented rather than a cohesive manner. The prefrontal-limbic complex often recognizes an emotion before any particular memory is retrieved. For example, the smell of chocolate chip cookies baking in the oven may immediately evoke feelings of happiness and contentment. This positive emotional response may result from memories of happy times baking chocolate chip cookies for the holidays. However, the first reaction involves an emotion which in turn leads toward the memory. And that's what therapy is often about—helping a person to recover the memories associated with the emotions. The prefrontal cortex is most certainly the control center for your emotions. The Scriptures give us this assurance in II Timothy 1:7, "*For God has not given us the spirit of fear, but of power, and of love, and of a sound mind.*"

Emotions always reveal one's faith. They reveal our core beliefs about God, ourselves, and what is really important to us. If we struggle with anger, perhaps we believe that we can handle situations better than God can and that we have a better plan. Are we anxious and fearful? Perhaps our God is not wise enough to sort out the details or strong enough to handle any conflict. A stress-filled life can even cause us to develop a habit of losing control of our emotions. Emotional outbursts can significantly damage our relationships with God and with other people. Self-control is one of the fruits of the Spirit and God can give you the ability to manage your emotions wisely.

God is an emotional God and we have been created in His image. Scripture frequently ascribes changing emotions to God. At various times He is said to be grieved (Psalm 78:40), angry (Deuteronomy 1:37), pleased (1 Kings 3:10), joyful (Zephaniah 3:17), and moved by pity (Judges 2:18). Unlike human emotions however, God's love is unfailing, unwavering, and eternally constant. That fact alone ought to convince us that God's affections are not like human passions. We are told in Hebrews that we have a High Priest who can sympathize with our weaknesses and infirmities because He was tempted in every respect as we are, but He did not sin, (Hebrews 4:15). Sin and the messiness of living on earth has distorted our emotions and caused them to "run away" at times. It is imperative that we seek to reflect the character of God and His purity, even through our emotions. That's what our journey on earth is all about—"*to be conformed to the image of His Son,*" Romans 8:29. Fear, jealousy, anger, anxiety, frustration, guilt and shame can derail us from that purpose. That is why it's essential to spend time daily meditating on God's Word, growing closer to Him, and reflecting His attributes in our lives every day. We need to bring our worldview into alignment to what the Bible teaches about our emotional and spiritual condition. Focusing on the readings and meditations in Part II and applying them to specific areas in your life, will allow you to do just that! Be sure to journal your thoughts as well. Remember—our emotions, thoughts, and behaviors are all interconnected and form the basis of our emotional health.

FIVE SKILLS TO DEVELOP YOUR EMOTIONAL HEALTH

"All learning has an emotional base."
–Plato

EMOTIONAL INTELLIGENCE

Our emotional health is a major factor in managing our physical and spiritual health. Negative emotions such as fear or anger, can zap our mental energy and even the ability to concentrate. Activities such as reflective reading, prayer, journaling, or mindfulness become increasingly difficult if not impossible when our mental energy is depleted. Negative attitudes can lead to chronic stress, upsetting our body's hormonal balance as well as depleting the brain chemicals required for happiness. The result is often feelings of hopelessness and despair. Scientific research shows that negative emotions can also lead to physical health problems such as high blood pressure, cardiovascular disease, osteoporosis, a weakened immune system, increased infections, and digestive disorders. In addition, our emotional health can negatively impact our behaviors and relationships with others, including our spiritual relationship with God.

In 1995, Daniel Goleman popularized the theory of Emotional Intelligence (EI) which emphasizes the importance of self-awareness, self-management, social awareness, relationship skills, and responsible decision-making. His book was based on research going back to the 1970's by Howard Gardner, Peter Salovey, John Mayer, and others. EI may also be referred to as Emotional Quotient (EQ), social intelligence, interpersonal communications, and emotional resilience. Our Emotional Intelligence (EI) allows us to effectively manage change and stress in our lives and helps to build resilience. Resilience is our ability to cope with life's setbacks and be able to bounce back rather than fall apart.

Maintaining strong positive relationships with loved ones and friends helps to foster support in both good and bad times and helps to build resilience. Mary and Martha are two Biblical examples. They routinely reached out to others by being hospitable and opening their home (Luke 10:38). Their style of relating was very different with Martha busying herself with preparations while Mary was interacting with the guests. Mary sat at Jesus' feet and "anointed the Lord with fragrant oil and wiped His feet with her hair," (John 11:2) while Martha was busy serving (Luke 10:40). However, the outcome for both women was similar. When an emotional crisis came into their lives after the death of their brother Lazarus, a support system was available to help them. The Bible tells us that the "Jews had joined the women around Mary and Martha, to comfort them concerning their brother." (John 11:19) They were not left alone to handle their grief in isolation. Their immediate circle of women friends surrounded them as well as the larger spiritual community to help foster emotional resilience. In addition, contrary to His disciples' advice, Jesus went back to Judea to Mary and Martha's house even though it potentially put His life in danger (John 11:8). He grieved right alongside the two women, groaning in His spirit and even weeping. Building strong positive relationships with loved ones and friends can help to build our emotional health.

Research has shown that positive emotions broaden our perspective of the world and actually build up over time. They inspire creativity and wonder and help us to see our options. Positive emotions also create lasting emotional resilience or the ability to experience tough emotions like pain, sorrow, frustration, and grief without falling apart. Resilience is like a rubber band—no matter how far you are stretched by negative experiences; you are able to bounce back. Forgiveness and gratitude are the foundations for developing emotional well-being.

FORGIVENESS

Many spiritual faiths, including Christianity, Judaism, Islam, and Buddhism teach the practice of letting go of blame and negative feelings after a hurtful incident. Modern science has shown that the health benefits of forgiveness are numerous including better immune function, longer lifespan, lowered blood pressure, improved cardiovascular health, and fewer feelings of anger or hurt. Forgiveness is often a slow process. It goes beyond simply telling someone, "I forgive you." Rather *forgiveness involves fully accepting a negative circumstance that has occurred and letting go of the negative feelings that surround the event.* That is why when Peter asked *"Should I forgive my brother up to seven times?"* that Jesus responded, *"I do not say to you, up to seven times, but up to seventy times seven,"* (Matthew 18:22). It can be very difficult, but forgiveness can be learned and will result in better emotional, physical, and spiritual health.

Forgiveness is a prominent theme in the Bible. Two types of forgiveness are mentioned: God's pardon of our sins, and our obligation to pardon others. I John 1:9 says, *"If we confess our sins, He is faithful and just to forgive us our sins and to cleanse us from all unrighteousness."* God's forgiveness towards us is based on the death of His Son, the Lord Jesus Christ—the atoning sacrifice for our sins. Romans 5:8 says, *"But God demonstrates His own love toward us, in that while we were still sinners, Christ died for us."* Many of us struggle with forgiveness since we don't naturally overflow with mercy, grace, and understanding toward those who have wronged us. However, I believe that the Bible teaches that *forgiveness is a choice we make through a decision of our will.* Our motivation is to obey God's command to forgive. Colossians 3:13 instructs us to *"bear with one another, and forgive one another, if anyone has a complaint against another; even as Christ forgave you, so you also must do."* In his book *Forgive and Forget,* Lewis B. Smedes wrote, *"When you release the wrongdoer from the wrong, you cut a malignant tumor out of your inner life. You set a prisoner free, but you discover that the real prisoner was yourself."* We must continue to forgive until the situation is settled in our heart. Only then will you be set free to develop your emotional health.

If forgiveness is so good for us, why do so many people choose not to forgive when they are hurt by someone? I believe that perhaps they have never been taught *how* to forgive. Most religions teach the importance of forgiveness but do not offer practical steps on how to do it. In fact, our culture often prizes resentment and "getting even" over love and forgiveness. Forgiveness involves healing ourselves from the emotional and physical pain which may have hurt us. It does not mean, however, condoning the wrongdoing. It also doesn't mean that we necessarily have to reconcile with someone who has treated us badly. Domestic violence and childhood abuse are two situations in which we may choose to forgive the offender but also choose to end or limit contact. The goal of forgiveness is to create peace of mind and help us to regain trust.

The Stanford Forgiveness Project trained 260 adults in forgiveness in a 6-week course. The results showed that 70% reported a decrease in their feelings of hurt, 13% experienced reduced anger, and 27% experienced fewer physical complaints such as pain, gastrointestinal upset, and dizziness. According to the Stanford Forgiveness Project, there are nine steps to forgiveness. I have also added appropriate Scripture verses as guidance.

9 STEPS TO FORGIVENESS

1. Identify and be able to articulate your feelings about the situation. Share your thoughts with a trusted friend. *"Just as iron sharpens iron, friends sharpen the minds of each other," Proverbs 27:17 Contemporary English Version (CEV).*

2. Make a commitment to do whatever it takes to feel better. Forgiveness is for you, no one else. *"Behold, You desire truth in the inward parts, And in the hidden part You will make me to know wisdom,"* Psalm 51:6.

3. Change your grievance story. Take the situation less personally. *"You meant evil against me; but God meant it for good,"* Genesis 50:20.

4. Realize that your primary distress is coming from hurt feelings and thoughts NOT what offended you or hurt you. The goal of forgiveness is to heal those hurt feelings. *"For the word of God is living and powerful, and sharper than any two-edged sword, piercing even to the division of soul and spirit, and of joints and marrow, and is a discerner of the thoughts and intents of the heart,"* Hebrews 4:12.

5. When you feel upset, practice a simple stress management technique. You can find examples and how to do them in the chapter on Brain Strain and Your Emotional Health. *"My eyes are awake through the night watches, that I may meditate on Your word,"* Psalm 119:148.

6. Let go of expecting things from other people that they don't choose to give you. You have no control over how other people must behave. *"My soul, wait silently for God alone, for my expectation is from Him,"* Psalm 62:5.

7. Instead of playing out your hurt, put your energy into finding how you can use the thing that hurt you to reach positive personal goals. *"And whatever you do, do it heartily, as to the Lord and not to men,"* Colossians 3:23.

8. Forgiveness is about personal power. Don't focus on your wounded feelings, giving the person who caused you pain to have power over you. Rather decide to live your life positively, looking for kindness, love, and beauty. *"Finally, brethren, whatever things are true, whatever things are noble, whatever things are just, whatever things are pure, whatever things are lovely, whatever things are of good report, if there is any virtue and if there is anything praiseworthy—meditate on these things,"* Philippians 4:8.

9. Remind yourself of the heroic choice to forgive. *". . .Choose for yourselves this day whom you will serve. . ."* Joshua 24:15.

GRATITUDE

The second foundational component for developing emotional health is gratitude or thankfulness. When you acknowledge the good aspects of life and give thanks, you will enhance your emotional wellness. Dr. Brene Brown, PhD, and licensed social worker, spent many years researching the relationship between joy and gratitude. What she discovered was an interesting twist. Logic would imply that joy leads to gratitude. However, what Dr. Brown's research revealed is just the opposite: *it's not joy that makes us grateful, but gratitude that makes us joyful.* Another landmark study showed that people who were asked to count their blessings felt happier, exercised more, had fewer physical complaints, and slept better than those who created lists of hassles. Do you focus on the hassles or do you count your blessings? Why not take a moment to reflect upon the words to the old hymn, *Count Your Blessings.*

Count Your Blessings

Lyrics by: Johnson Oatman Jr.

When upon life's billows you are tempest-tossed,
When you are discouraged, thinking all is lost,
Count your many blessings, name them one by one,
And it will surprise you what the Lord hath done.

Refrain:
Count your blessings, name them one by one,
Count your blessings, see what God hath done!
Count your blessings, name them one by one,
Count your many blessings, see what God hath done.

Are you ever burdened with a load of care?
Does the cross seem heavy you are called to bear?
Count your many blessings, every doubt will fly,
And you will keep singing as the days go by.

When you look at others with their lands and gold,
Think that Christ has promised you His wealth untold;
Count your many blessings—money cannot buy
Your reward in heaven, nor your home on high.

So, amid the conflict whether great or small,
Do not be discouraged, God is over all;
Count your many blessings, angels will attend,
Help and comfort give you to your journey's end.

"Giving thanks always for all things to God the Father in the name of our Lord Jesus Christ," Ephesians 5:20.

The Collaborative for Academic, Social, and Emotional Learning (CASEL) defines five areas that impact our social and emotional learning. Their scientific work relates primarily to students but can be applied to anyone. Our emotional health depends on our skill in each of these five areas.

SELF-AWARENESS

Self-awareness is the first skill to understand our emotions and how they influence our behaviors. Ask the question, "What is driving my behavior? Am I making conscious choices or am I simply reacting?" There are several ways to improve our self-awareness. Mindfulness can be a great tool. Mindfulness simply means being fully present rather than distracted by the many things competing for our attention. Taking ourselves off auto-pilot or cruise control allows things to slow down. Mindfulness is simply a particular way of paying attention to present-moment experiences. From ancient times the Bible has stressed the importance of being quiet and waiting on God. The Psalmist tells us, "*Surely I have calmed and quieted my soul,*" Psalm 131:2. The initiative begins with us. We need to find a special place where we can be alone with God every day—away from the distractions of the Internet, television, cell phones and even other family members. It may be a chair in your bedroom or even sitting alone in your car. Sometimes the only place may be the bathroom! What does it mean to "calm and quiet our soul?" We are told in Zephaniah 3:17 that "*The Lord your God, The Mighty One . . . will quiet you with His love,*" Once we make a conscious choice to practice mindfulness, God steps in to actively work on our behalf. The all-powerful, eternal, all-knowing "*shows Himself active on behalf of him who [earnestly] waits for Him,*" Isaiah 64:4 AMP.

MINDFUL BREATHING

One great way to quiet ourselves before the Lord is to take five minutes and simply focus on our breathing. This is a great technique to prepare ourselves before opening God's word or spending time in prayer. If five minutes seems to be too long at first, try it for two minutes. Mindfulness breathing is not necessarily relaxation breathing or stress reduction breathing, although that may occur. Rather, it is simply noticing and becoming aware of your breath. It may be difficult at first to simply be present in the moment, feeling the hardness or softness of the surface where you are seated or lying down, and noticing your breath as it moves into your nostrils and through your body and then out again. It is helpful to close your eyes to remove other distractions. Bring all your attention to the physical act of breathing. It doesn't matter if it is slow or fast, deep or shallow. Breathing is something we carry with us everywhere; however, we are not usually aware of it. If other thoughts intrude, just notice them and then gently bring your attention back to your breathing. With practice, mindful breathing will become more comfortable and will help you to develop a greater self-awareness as you allow the Holy Spirit to communicate with your spirit. (Romans 8:16)

MINDFUL LISTENING

Mindful listening is another technique to help increase our self-awareness. Close your eyes and pay attention to the sounds that you hear around you. Perhaps it's the clock ticking in your room or the fan or air conditioner blowing. Maybe it's the birds singing outside, the rain pelting on the window, or even the ocean crashing on the beach. Let the sounds that you hear take "center stage" as you become more aware of your surroundings. Some people enjoy reverently listening to a quiet piece of instrumental music to quiet themselves and increase self-awareness.

MINDFUL WRITING

Finally, mindful writing or journaling is another tool to help gain perspective. Some people enjoy using a composition book with colored flair tip pens to express their feelings. However, a Smartphone, tablet, or computer works just as well for those who must stick to using only technology. Journaling provides an opportunity for us to reflect on our emotions by capturing the words that describe our feelings. It allows us to process emotional experiences when we are better able to think about them on a conscious level. The brain can produce emotional responses that impact our behavior directly in the amygdala, bypassing the analytical part of our brain known as the prefrontal cortex. Self-awareness is the first skill to understand our emotions and how they influence our behaviors. Ask the question, "What is driving my behavior? Am I making conscious choices or am I simply reacting? Am I manipulating my circumstances to reach my goals or do I believe that God 'acts for the one who waits for Him?'" (Isaiah 64:4) Try to clarify the barriers to responding to an interaction with another person in an emotionally appropriate manner. Describe the interaction from the perspective of the other person. What did they think of you? After taking time to explore the feelings, notice any changes in how you feel. Has breathing slowed down and become deeper? Has emotional balance been restored or maintained? Take a moment to just enjoy that feeling.

In Part II of this book, you will find selected mindfulness readings that focus on the various fruit of the Spirit. Select two or three entries on which to focus your attention each day. Meditate on the Scriptures and prayerfully consider what the words are saying and how they apply to your life. Be specific and record your thoughts. As you do, you will develop an increased self-awareness and identify those areas in your life that need "pruning." *My Mindful Journal* is a helpful tool to assist in gaining self-awareness and setting goals to develop spiritual growth.

SELF-MANAGEMENT—TRACK YOUR PROGRESS BY JOURNALING

Self-management is another core skill for emotional health. It is essential to ensure that our response is appropriate to the situation. The goal of self-management is to develop the ability to regulate our emotions, thoughts, and behaviors in different situations, particularly during stressful times. Do others observe you as calm and patient even during challenging situations? Motivation, setting and achieving personal goals, controlling our impulses, and generally managing stress are all components of self-management. An effective way to monitor our self-management is to keep track of any impulsive reactions. What did the reaction look like? What was happening right before the reaction? What were you doing or thinking about? What were the emotional triggers? What were the results? Look for patterns and choose a better response instead of feeling out of control. Add these responses to your journal so that you can track your progress in self-management. Set personal goals with specific target dates. Be sure that your goals are measurable so that you can evaluate your progress. For example, if you have a goal to lose weight, define a specific target weight and when and how you expect to reach it. What lifestyle changes do you need to make? What are the changes needed in your diet and activity level? How will you monitor and track your progress? How often will you evaluate your results and modify your plan? While you may be tempted to simply set and review personal goals mentally, it is far more effective to write them down and develop a specific action plan to reach your target.

SOCIAL AWARENESS

Understanding other people's feelings is a third essential skill for emotional health. The starting place for becoming socially aware is self-awareness and self-management is necessary to ensure that our response is appropriate. A major component of social awareness is empathy or the ability to grasp another person's needs, emotions, and concerns and then communicate with them in a way that will help to meet those needs. Learning how to take the perspective of others and empathize with them expands our ability to interact with Emotional Intelligence (EI).

The more we learn about others, the more we will develop the skill of social awareness. An empathetic response requires awareness of diversity as well as sensitivity to the emotions and needs of others. It includes respect for individual differences, open communication, and the recognition of individual differences and uniqueness.

Improving our listening skills is an important way to build social awareness. Pay close attention to interactions with other people and notice how they are responding to others such as someone greeting them or asking them something. Be aware of what they say, how they say it, and what they do. Remember James 1:19, "Be swift to hear, slow to speak, slow to wrath." Think about your feelings. How does the other person's emotion make you feel? How did you change your body language, facial expressions and tone of voice to demonstrate empathy for the other person? Did you ask questions about not only the content but the feelings and emotions of what was being said?

Consider learning about a cultural group that is different from yours. Identify their customs, food, dress, and religious practices. A practical approach to finding out about other cultural groups is to correspond with a missionary or someone you may know who is living in another country. This is a great way to discover first-hand about their cultural experiences. If there are different cultural groups where you live, make it a point to become aware of their specific practices so that you can empathize and interact appropriately.

In South Florida, we have a large Haitian population. French and Creole are the two official languages of Haiti but Creole is the national language used by the entire population. Haitians are very expressive and tend to get loud and use hand gestures when discussing topics of interest, such as politics. They are very friendly and embrace and kiss as a sign of affection and acceptance in informal situations. Various home remedies are the first choice for treating illnesses rather than conventional treatment. Although Roman Catholicism is the primary religion, voodoo is still taken very seriously which is important to consider when interacting with people from Haiti.

A big cultural issue is that they are not committed to time or a schedule which can be frustrating since it is not considered impolite to arrive late for an event or appointment. My husband and I had friends who were perpetually late for gatherings of any type, sometimes up to two hours. One weekend, we invited our friends to come for dinner and I thought that I had it all figured out. I gave our guests an arrival time of one hour earlier than I had planned. Were we ever embarrassed when amazingly this couple showed up "on time" and I still hadn't showered or dressed! Needless to say, we all had a good laugh. By increasing your social awareness about various cultural groups in your particular area, you will be better able to understand them, interact appropriately, and empathize with their concerns.

RELATIONSHIP SKILLS

Relationship skills are the fourth skill set for emotional health. Maintaining strong social relationships is a well-founded predictor of the sustainability of wellness for both men and women, according to the HEALTH Factor. Research has shown that loneliness contributes to numerous physical and emotional health consequences including:

- Depression and suicide
- Cardiovascular disease and stroke
- Increased stress levels
- Decreased memory and learning
- Antisocial behavior
- Poor decision-making
- Alcoholism and drug abuse
- Progression of Alzheimer's disease
- Altered brain function

A woman's brain circuits are fueled by estrogen to respond to stress by creating protective social networks and initiating nurturing behaviors. Oxytocin, the hormone of bonding, also plays a significant role. What we know is that females react more to relationship stresses and males to challenges to their authority.

The need to belong and the desire for interpersonal attachments are a fundamental human motivation according to the research of Roy F. Baumeister of Case Western Reserve University and Mark R. Leary of Wake Forest University. *"Belongingness appears to have multiple and strong effects on emotional patterns and on cognitive processes. Lack of attachments is linked to a variety of ill effects on health, adjustment, and well-being."* In 1968, Abraham Maslow, an American psychologist, ranked "love and belongingness" in the middle of his hierarchy of human needs. According to Maslow, this need to belong does not surface until the more basic needs of food, shelter, and safety are met. However, it emerges before self-esteem and self-actualization.

Regardless of your opinion about *Maslow's Hierarchy of Needs*, God identified the human need of love and belongingness as far back as the Garden of Eden. The Torah records that ADONAI, God, said, *"It isn't good that the person should be alone. I will make for him a companion suitable for helping him."* (Genesis 2:18 CJB). *"There's a social science adage that the strongest predictor of well-being in men is being married, and in women it's having female friends,"* says University of Alberta professor Kathleen Hegadoren, RN, PhD. *"Female relationships are important, and you need to take the time and effort to sustain them,"* according to Dr. Hegadoren.

One example of sustaining female relationships is found in the New Testament, between Mary, the mother of Jesus, and her cousin Elizabeth, John the Baptist's mother. When Mary found out that she was pregnant, she immediately went to share the news with Elizabeth, who was also pregnant, and ended up spending three months with her (Luke 1:39-56). I can only imagine what they might have talked about and planned together in those three months! Do you have a small circle of friends with whom you can share intimate moments?

The research supports that it is not the quantity but the quality of social connections that is important to maintaining good health. Dr. John Cacioppo is a pioneer in the field of social neuroscience and an expert in social isolation, emotional contagion, and social behavior. He is the Director of the Center for Cognitive and Social Neuroscience at the University of Chicago. In his book *Loneliness: Human Nature and the Need for Social Connection* he not only describes the origins and implications for loneliness but provides a step-by-step approach to reducing your own loneliness which is grounded in good science.

Establishing and maintaining healthy relationships with other individuals and groups is built upon knowing how to communicate effectively. Actively listening, negotiating conflict appropriately, and seeking and offering help to others all help build emotional and social strength. The Bible tells us in James 1:19, "Let every man be swift to hear, slow to speak, slow to wrath." When someone is speaking, really listen to what he or she is saying rather than thinking about your response. Think about the feeling behind people's words and give them some verbal feedback to indicate that you heard them/listened carefully. Ask appropriate questions about what is important in their lives to encourage positive communication.

Assertive versus either passive or aggressive communication is an important skill to learn because it is built on mutual respect. Assertive communication helps us to understand and recognize our feelings as well as create honest relationships. Here are some tips to help you to develop an assertive communication style:

Understand your personal style of communication: Do you always voice your opinions or do you tend to remain silent? Do others see you as boisterous and loud? Do you have a hard time saying no to additional responsibilities even if your schedule is full? Are you quick to judge or blame others? Assess your own style of communication to determine if it is passive, assertive, or aggressive.

Use "I" statements: Let others know directly what you are thinking rather than using a "you" statement which sounds accusatory. For example, "I disagree" versus "You're wrong."

Practice saying no: If this is a problem area for you, try to say, "No, I can't do that now." Keep your explanations brief.

Rehearse what you want to say: Practice saying or writing out your responses to particularly difficult encounters. You may even want to role-play with a friend.

Be aware of your body language: Non-verbal communication is very powerful. Act confident even if you're not. Make good eye contact and avoid excessive hand movements and gestures. Smile appropriately and look pleasant. Keep your voice even and firm.

RESPONSIBLE DECISION MAKING

We face decisions every day, some more difficult than others. It is important to remember that there may not always be a "correct" decision among the choices; however, there are a few basic guidelines to follow when making a decision:

1. List all the possible solutions or options
2. Gather information about each one
3. Consider the risks involved
4. Prioritize the choices based on what is important
5. Weigh the pros and cons of each option
6. Make the decision

Responsible decision-making involves evaluating the consequences of our actions on both ourselves and others. Our choices about our own personal behavior as well as how we interact with others need to be respectful, wise, and based on ethical standards and safety concerns. Proverbs 3:5-6 tells us, *"Trust in the Lord with all your heart, and lean not on your own understanding; in all your ways acknowledge Him, and He shall direct your paths."*

BRAIN STRAIN SABOTAGES EMOTIONAL HEALTH - IS YOUR BRAIN ON STRIKE?

"The greatest weapon against stress is our ability to choose one thought over another." –William James

Over the long haul, the brain mobilizes all the hormone systems to help us cope with issues such as financial problems, a poor marriage, loneliness and social isolation, chronic low self-esteem, caring for sick family members, and on and on. New scientific research has also identified how chronic stress can actually decrease our lifespan! Our telomeres, or the "end caps" of our DNA strands, are shortened by chronic stress. These telomeres play a major role in the aging process.

Stress looks very different today than how it looked in the past. Today, a pneumonia infection means taking an antibiotic or possibly a short hospital stay. In the past, however, it often meant death! Likewise weather conditions, travel, food, and housing were all significant acute stressors. They were mostly survival issues that could be settled relatively quickly by getting our muscles moving. Today, however, our stressors tend to be more chronic in nature—hectic workplaces, financial concerns, chaotic families, where to go to school, retirement planning, etc. If stress hormones are elevated for too long, they become harmful.

In the late 1960's psychologist Martin Seligman PhD coined the phrase "learned helplessness." When we no longer are able to see any options in a situation and we develop the perception of inescapability, learning is shut down and chronic stress occurs. Sometimes, however, it is difficult to determine when someone is experiencing stress. To us, an explorer climbing Mount Everest in a blizzard with a limited food supply might be perceived as enduring an inordinate amount of stress when in fact he may be energized by the experience. In the brain, stress and pleasure look the same physiologically. Whether shaking in fear and horror or enjoying a fabulous meal with good friends, our brain records it the same way.

According to Jeansok Kim and David Diamond, three components must be present for stress to occur:

1. An aroused physiologic response measured by an outside party, i.e. shouting, shaking, crying, etc.
2. An aversive stressor—an unpleasant situation that the person wants to avoid
3. Loss of control resulting in "learned helplessness." The greater the loss of control, the more severe the stress is perceived to be.

Stress can be triggered by a range of issues which may be physical, emotional or environmental. Did you know that inflammation, physical trauma, toxic exposure, poor sleep, and illness can all trigger the stress response? Even imagined events can have a profound physical impact on our bodies. People who suffer from anxiety and panic disorders can attest to that fact, being all too well acquainted with pounding heart rates, shortness of breath, sweaty palms, and jitteriness. Stressful situations, along with the emotions that accompany them, cause a significant effect on the stress pathways in our brain. They load the brain's self-regulatory systems and eventually deplete or throw the brain's coping mechanisms completely out of balance. That is why it is essential for us to monitor those factors which may be influencing our brain's stability. This dysregulation can occur either when the body is actually threatened or when it is perceived to be threatened.

The question is - when does the breaking point occur? Some people seem to have an inordinate amount of stress but somehow continue to cope with life. Let's use a seesaw to help to illustrate the concept of brain strain. Imagine continuing to add a heavier and heavier load to a seesaw. It may creak and groan as it goes up and down but finally, when the weight becomes too heavy, the seesaw will break. The breaking point is determined not only by the weight of the load but also the seesaw's intrinsic qualities: the strength of the wood, the maintenance of the equipment, and the resilience to the extremes of weather. In a similar fashion, a number of factors determine how a person's brain handles stress. A key component is a person's genetic susceptibility to mental illness—what was inherited as part of the brain's basic make up. People who are not genetically at risk are able to shut off the over secretion of stress hormones when they are no longer required. They are intrinsically more resilient. However, the good news is that in terms of brain maintenance, it is possible for a person to compensate for genetic risk factors by actively learning how to change their thinking by using cognitive and behavioral strategies. Your mind and your body are intertwined, and even though you may think that you are resting, taking a nap, putting your feet up, etc. your mind is generally on high alert.

When the strain overcomes the brain's capacity to compensate, the brain goes on strike! This process is called *allostatic loading*. Dr. Bruce McEwen, a neuroscientist at Rockefeller University in New York, coined this phrase. "Allostasis" refers to the body's ability to adapt when it is subjected to increased demands. Allo comes from the Greek word meaning variable; and stasis means a condition of balance. Our body's reaction to stress depends upon the stress itself, the length and severity of the stress, and on our body's ability to adapt.

There is an unevenness of human response to stress, sometimes referred to as stress-tolerance versus stress-sensitivity. Scientists who have studied resilience observed that those people who respond rapidly to stress with a surge of stress hormones but then recover quickly seem to cope better with stressful situations like a stressful job. More resilient people also seem to be better at using the hormone dopamine which has a role in the brain's reward system to help keep them positive during stress. Dennis Charney from the Icaln School of Medicine at Mount Sinai in New York City and Steven Southwick from the Yale School of Medicine have identified ten psychological and social factors that they think build strong resilience:

1. Facing fear
2. Having a moral compass
3. Drawing on faith
4. Using social support
5. Having good role models
6. Being physically fit
7. Making sure your brain is challenged
8. Having cognitive and emotional flexibility
9. Having meaning, purpose, and growth in life
10. Realistic optimism

Charney and Southwick believe that it is possible for relatively healthy people to develop these ten factors to help them cope with day-to-day life stressors. One technique that they have used successfully is called mindfulness. Although its origins are in the Zen Buddhist tradition, it has been completely secularized and Westernized to reflect its central ideas of attention and awareness. Mindfulness means paying attention, on purpose, in the present moment in a non-judgmental way. At its core, mindfulness is a stress reduction technique. It is about bringing awareness to thought. It is simplifying our thoughts not emptying our mind. What is "cleared" is the overwhelming majority of thoughts—**mindfulness teaches how to quiet**

the incessant dialogue that truly ravages our brain to then bring forth clarity and calm. The Psalmist says in Psalm 131:2, "Surely I have calmed and quieted my soul. . ." A key part of Christian mindfulness is to attentively listen to the Word of God and to the living Word, Christ Himself. What emerges is a new mind, not shaped by our old habitual ways of thinking, according to the patterns of this world, but by our new life in Christ. "Roll your works upon the Lord [commit and trust them wholly to Him; He will cause your thoughts to become agreeable to His will, and] so shall your plans be established and succeed," Proverbs 16:3 AMP. Attentiveness, awareness, and listening obedience are the core elements of Christian mindfulness. Part II of Your Mind Redefined along with My Mindful Journal provides a structured format to develop these skills.

WARNING SIGNS OF STRESS OVERLOAD

The warning signs of stress overload can show up as physical symptoms, behavioral symptoms, emotional symptoms, or cognitive symptoms. **Physical symptoms** include headaches, indigestion, stomachaches, sweaty palms, sleep difficulties, dizziness, back pain, tight neck and shoulders, racing heart, restlessness, tiredness, and ringing in your ears. **Behavioral symptoms** include bossiness, a critical attitude, overuse of alcohol, inability to get things done, compulsive eating, grinding teeth at night, compulsive gum chewing, and excess smoking. **Emotional symptoms** include crying, nervousness or anxiety, boredom, feeling ready to explode, powerlessness, overwhelming sense of pressure, anger, loneliness, unhappiness for no reason, and easily upset. **Cognitive symptoms** include forgetfulness, inability to make decisions, trouble thinking clearly, loss of sense of humor, constant worry, thoughts of running away, lack of creativity, and memory loss.

Do any of these seem familiar? We all react to stress differently, but if we don't find ways to de-stress either through exercise or some other type of relaxation strategy, the continued high level of excitement causes wear and tear on our bodies which leads to illness! Monitoring our sleep, memory and concentration, as well as overall stress levels can help us be aware that brain strain can be impacting our overall health. The Bible gives us this promise in Isaiah 26:3, *"You will keep him in perfect peace, whose mind is stayed on You, because he trusts in You."*

Our mind has a powerful influence over our physical health and well-being. Just a reminder that the Bible confirmed this fact thousands of years ago in the book of Proverbs 22:7, *"As he thinks in his heart, so is he."* Therefore, it is essential to guard our mind. The Lord Jesus says in Revelation 2:23, *"I am He who searches the minds and hearts."* When we actively seek to align our thinking with God's, we are told that *"the peace of God, which surpasses all understanding, will guard your hearts and minds through Christ Jesus."* Philippians 4:7. Since stress has been found to be linked to depression, be sure to track your mood on a regular basis. The Center for Epidemiological Studies Depression screening (CES-D) is an easy way to track depression symptoms. This screening tool can be found online.

THE STRESS RESPONSE AND THE HPA AXIS—HYPOTHALAMUS, PITUITARY, ADRENAL AXIS

The Hypothalamic-Pituitary-Adrenal (HPA) Axis is a signaling route that controls the stress response. It starts in our brain but it affects the entire body. In the brain it extends from the hypothalamus to the pituitary gland and then continues on to the adrenal gland which sits above our kidneys. Our brain controls this elaborate feedback loop that starts off in the hypothalamus, causing it to release a hormone known as corticotrophin-releasing hormone (CRH). CRH is then transported to the pituitary gland which then secretes another hormone, adrenocorticotropic hormone (ACTH). ACTH then stimulates the adrenal gland to releases the stress hormone cortisol. A negative feedback loop is set up meaning that high levels of cortisol trigger the hypothalamus to reduce its output of CRH which in turn lowers the levels of ACTH and cortisol. (See Appendix III: Cortisol Controlled by the HPA Axis—A Negative Feedback Loop) So cortisol serves two purposes in our body - as both the primary stress hormone and as the primary anti-stress hormone. For years researchers have known that depression is associated with elevated levels of cortisol. What we now know is that in people with depression, the HPA axis is unable to turn itself off and therefore releases more and more cortisol. The reason for this is that the sensitivity of the glucocorticoid receptors for cortisol is decreased in people with depression.

CORTISOL—THE GOOD, THE BAD, AND THE UGLY

Cortisol is a life-sustaining adrenal hormone, but long-term surges associated with chronic stress can be deadly. Most of the stress we face today is not life threatening. There really isn't a tiger or a bear running after us. However, physical stress from a car accident, infection, or surgery; emotional stress following the death of a loved one or news of a terminal illness; or environmental stress from consuming too much enriched or processed food or sugary drinks, or being exposed to extreme weather conditions are all examples of acute stress. Here is how cortisol helps us handle acute stress:

- It normalizes your blood sugar level: Cortisol works in tandem with insulin, which is released from the pancreas, to provide adequate glucose to your body's cells to use for energy. Additional energy from any source is required when the body is under stress, and cortisol is the hormone that makes this happens. This action helps you to run fast and think quickly. Cortisol is a catabolic hormone - it will break tissue down in your bones, muscles, and liver. It utilizes the glucose that you've stored up to assure adequate fuel to keep you functioning at a higher level during times of acute stress. It also pulls calcium from your bones making it available to muscles for immediate action.
- It is a powerful anti-inflammatory agent whose objective is to remove and prevent swelling and redness in nearly all tissues.
- It suppresses the immune system: People with high cortisol levels are very much weaker from the immunological point of view. Cortisol suppresses white blood cells, natural killer cells, monocytes, macrophages, and mast cells. It prevents the immune system from becoming overzealous and destructive in the short-term.
- It contracts mid-size arteries and increases blood flow to your muscles, brain, and heart so that these organs can perform more efficiently. Conversely, people with low cortisol levels (as in advanced stages of Adrenal Dysfunction) have low blood pressure and reduced reactivity to other body agents that will constrict blood vessels.

Although cortisol provides many benefits, when it is released in excess, or for a prolonged period of time, it can create many pathological conditions in the body. Chronic stressful situations such as daily job stress, financial insecurity, obesity, and environmental toxins result in chronic cortisol elevation. The levels of cortisol in your body never get a chance to return to normal. This chronic elevation produces a major threat to your health. The problems associated with chronically elevated cortisol levels include:

- Lowered immune function
- Hypertension or high blood pressure
- High blood sugar (hyperglycemia)
- Insulin resistance and blood sugar imbalances
- Carbohydrate cravings

- Metabolic syndrome and type 2 diabetes
- Fat deposits on the face, neck, and belly
- Reduced libido
- Bone loss
- Insomnia or sleep disruption
- Impaired cognitive performance
- Low thyroid function
- Decreased muscle mass
- Slow wound healing

The effects of chronic overexposure to cortisol can be devastating! When cortisol levels remain high, our blood sugar levels stay elevated resulting in increased cravings for sweets and carbohydrates. There is often a substantial loss of calcium from our bones, leading to osteopenia or osteoporosis. When cortisol is chronically high, our immune system does not function well and we become more susceptible to infections. Did you ever notice that when you are stressed you tend to catch more colds and other viruses? At first, stress equips our white blood cells (WBCs) to fight infections. However, chronic stress actually decreases the number of WBCs and attacks the part of the immune system responsible for producing antibodies to fight infections. Studies have shown that we are more vulnerable if the stressors are social in nature and lasted more than a month.

High blood pressure is another problem from chronically elevated cortisol causing vasoconstriction or narrowing of blood vessels, making it more difficult for blood to pass through without increased pressure. Chronic stress has also been shown to create sandpaper-like rough spots on the inside wall of our arteries. These spots can turn to scars which allow plaque to build up there and eventually clog our arteries. The result is in an increased risk of heart attacks and strokes. Sustained high cortisol also causes us to lose muscle mass because it breaks down muscle for energy. Fat accumulates in our abdominal area and we may even experience foggy thinking and depression.

Our brain is also very responsive to chronic stress stress signals. According to John Medina in *Brain Rules*, the hippocampus is "studded with cortisol receptors like cloves in a ham." Stress hormones have a particular liking to cells in the hippocampus where human learning occurs. They can disconnect the networks of neurons, stop the birth of new neurons and even kill brain cells under extreme conditions. Stressful experiences form memories almost instantaneously which can be recalled very quickly during times of crisis. However, severe or prolonged stress actually interferes with both short and long-term memory, decreases our ability to problem-solve, and prevents us from processing language and math very well. Brain

Derived Neurotrophic Factor (BDNF) is part of a powerful group of proteins called neurotrophins. BDNF keeps neurons alive and growing and prevents stress hormones from doing their damage. However, too many stress hormones over a prolonged period of time can actually turn off the gene that makes BDNF resulting in forgetfulness and depression.

If the timing of cortisol secretion is off balance, insomnia or sleep disruption can occur. Cortisol is generally highest around 8:00 a.m. with a gradual decline throughout the day. It is at its lowest between midnight and 4:00 a.m. When cortisol is chronically elevated for a long time, the communication between our brain and adrenals becomes skewed. If this happens, the cortisol output can be too low or secreted at inappropriate times, such as at 2:00 or 3:00 a.m., when it should be low. This surge in the middle of the night can result in the inability to stay asleep all night.

Eventually, our adrenal glands can't sustain the high cortisol levels. So what started out as the protective stress response begins to undermine and exhaust us, as we remain perpetually hyper-vigilant chemically. When adrenal output starts to fall, the result is fatigue, depression, apathy, increased respiratory infections due to compromised immunity, and a generalized decrease in well-being.

If you've ever seen someone on chronic steroid therapy, such as for systemic vasculitis - inflammation of blood vessels - or rheumatoid arthritis - inflammatory arthritis occurring in the joints - you may have seen some of the destructive effects of cortisol such as the classic "moon face," which is the result of excess fat and fluid accumulations. The individual may have developed a stooped posture, the result of calcium losses from the bones. People on chronic steroid therapy often succumb to infections as a result of excessive immune suppression. Also, they often develop dangerous hypertension or high blood pressure requiring medication. In addition, they can develop a range of brain or cognitive dysfunctions feeling which cause them to feel depressed, irritable, or anxious. They may even develop psychosis, a serious thought disorder. The range of symptoms generally relates to how high the dose of the steroid and how long a person has been taking it.

Studies have shown that some people have a more sensitive HPA axis which can be set off by only minor triggers. When this happens, we may have difficulty turning off the HPA axis in an efficient way. Severe chronic stress can wreak extraordinary changes in our bodies, minds, and behavior. High circulating cortisol levels can damage our brain neurons and lower our thyroid function, adding to feelings of fatigue. **As cortisol increases due to physical, emotional, or environmental stress, not only do thyroid hormones decrease but inflammation increases.** This inflammation can lead to various physical health problems including increased cholesterol, increased plaque formation, increased blood pressure, heart disease, diabetes, cancer, and various autoimmune diseases such as osteoporosis, rheumatoid arthritis, Crones Disease, irritable bowel syndrome (IBS), and fibromyalgia. The new science of stress also links depression to chronic brain inflammation.

Monitor and track your blood pressure on a daily basis using one of the many apps available. If you are experiencing chronic stress, have your healthcare provider monitor your CRP (C-reactive protein) as well as IL-6 (Interlukin-6) an inflammatory marker. In addition, monitor your cholesterol levels since cortisol is made from cholesterol. If cholesterol is high, there's a good chance that your cortisol levels are high as well. You can monitor your cortisol levels directly by checking your salivary cortisol levels. There are a number of reputable sources on the internet that offer this type of testing including ZRT and Labric Laboratories as well as Life Extension. Finally, be sure that your healthcare provider monitors your thyroid levels since as cortisol increases, thyroid levels decrease which could be a reason for feelings of fatigue.

Science has shown us that there is also a relationship between obesity, stress, and depression. Obesity can lead to metabolic syndrome, insulin resistance, and ultimately diabetes if left unchecked! If our stress levels are elevated, it is crucial to monitor our weight, basal metabolic rate (BMR), fasting blood glucose levels, and the glycemic index or glycemic load of the foods we regularly consume to keep our weight in check. Since chronic elevated stress levels have been shown to be associated with both obesity and depression, routine monitoring can help us keep our weight on track.

ADRENAL GLANDS—THE PHARMACY OF THE BODY

The endpoint of the HPA axis is the adrenal glands. They are about the size of a walnut and weigh no more than a grape. However, they affect the functioning of every single tissue, organ, and gland in our body. The adrenal glands play an important role in fluid balance and help to regulate our blood sugar. They influence how we think and feel and determine how our immune system is working. When the adrenals are out of balance, the quality of our health and well-being deteriorates. It is interesting to note that God designed our bodies with two blood filters about the size of a fist that filter six quarts of blood every 20 minutes; the adrenal glands sit on top of each of these filters. Can you think of any better location for such an important gland? The adrenals keep our body's reaction to stress in balance to ensure that those reactions are appropriate and not harmful. They manufacture and secrete almost fifty different hormones including more than fifteen steroid hormones such as adrenalin, cortisol, aldosterone, estrogen, and progesterone. These hormones convert from one to another in an elaborate system known as the steroid hormone cascade. (See Appendix II: The Steroid Hormone Cascade) Interestingly, the one building material is cholesterol.

Cholesterol levels and cortisol are closely linked. In fact, much of the current research today demonstrates the impact of stress as a risk factor for heart disease, diabetes, and autoimmune diseases. Because cortisol is essential to life, an important phenomenon occurs in the steroid hormone cascade. Instead of one hormone "neatly" converting to the next hormone in the cascade, something called "*pregnenolone steal*" occurs. All the hormones in the steroid cascade "defer" to cortisol. Cholesterol bypasses all the other hormones, including progesterone, and immediately is used as the building block for cortisol. When we're under stress, progesterone decreases significantly in favor of cortisol causing progesterone to almost "bottom out." Can you see how high cholesterol can relate to high stress levels? **As more cortisol is needed, cholesterol increases to meet the demand.**

As we age, our hormone reserves and our ability to produce hormones decline for both men and women. Hormone levels in a 40-year-old are often less than 50% of the levels of a 20-year-old. For women, menopause brings about an increased demand on the adrenals because the ovaries' ability to produce progesterone falls sharply. The slack is then taken up by the adrenal glands which are now also responsible for taking over the production of sex hormones. It's no wonder that perimenopause and menopause can be devastating for women with adrenal dysfunction!

Cortisol is the most potent hormone produced in the adrenal cortex when the body is under physical, emotional, or chemical stress. Without cortisol, a person has a condition known as Addison's disease, or adrenal failure, and must take cortisol to survive. Unfortunately, the blood test for checking the adrenal glands does not show any abnormalities until about 90% of the adrenals have shut down!

BRAIN STRAIN AND YOUR THOUGHTS

The new science of stress demonstrates that how you think about stress is what matters. A study in 2012 at the University of Wisconsin tracked 30,000 adults in the United States for eight years. The participants were asked two questions:

1. How much stress have you experienced in the last year?
2. Do you believe that stress is harmful to your health?

The researchers then used public health records to find out who died. The bad news was that people who experienced a lot of stress had a 43% risk of dying, but that was only true of the people who also believed that stress is harmful to their health. The people who experienced a lot of stress but did not believe it was harmful were no more likely to die—in fact, they had the lowest risk of dying of anyone in the study including people who had relatively little stress! Over 182,000 people died, not from stress, but from the belief that stress is bad for us. That number resulted in more than 22,000 deaths per year making it the 15th leading cause of death. **Those individuals who had the lowest risk of dying from the effects of stress saw stress as a sign that the body was being energized to handle the problem rather than having trouble coping.** When we change the way that we think about stress, our body's response to stress changes. This is the new science of stress.

Another study conducted at Harvard University found similar results. When individuals were given a social stress test, those who responded positively saw their body as helping them to rise to whatever challenge they were facing. Before taking the social stress test, the participants were taught to rethink their response to stress as helpful. Their pounding heart rate was preparing them for action. Their rapid breathing was getting more oxygen to the brain. However, the most fascinating response involved the blood vessels. During a typical stress response, our heart rate increases and our blood vessels constrict or get narrow. This action is one of the reasons why chronic stress can be associated with heart disease. It is definitely not healthy to constantly be in this type of physical state, putting a person at risk for hypertension, strokes, and heart attacks. However, in the study, **when participants viewed their stress response as helpful, their blood vessels remained relaxed. Their heart was pounding but their blood vessels did not constrict.** This physical state resembled what happens to the body during moments of joy or courage. This response could potentially make a huge difference in experiencing a stress-induced heart attack at 50 years old versus living disease free for many years.

A third important research study demonstrated that a person's stress response has a built-in mechanism for stress resilience called human connections. Oxytocin is a stress hormone that is pumped out by the pituitary gland in your brain during times of stress. Oxytocin's role is to make a person more social. It fine tunes our brain's social instincts, causes us to crave physical contact, increases our empathy, and makes us more willing to support others that we care about. Oxytocin acts on the brain and the body to protect us from the cardiovascular effects of stress. It is an anti-inflammatory neurohormone which helps the body to stay relaxed during times of stress. Our heart has receptors for this hormone and research demonstrates that it helps the heart cells to regenerate and heal from any stress-induced damage. **Oxytocin motivates us to seek support. This is another feedback loop in the body—a built-in mechanism for stress**

resilience. If you reach out to others when you are under stress, either to seek support or to help them, you release more of this hormone and actually recover faster from stress.

The new science of stress emphasizes that the harmful effects of stress are not inevitable. Positive stress management can be summarized by these two principles:

THINK: How we think about stress really matters. Conceptualize our stress reactions as our body's mechanism to help us rise to whatever challenges we may be experiencing. Create the biology of courage and joy by how we think. The Bible gives us a wonderful illustration about correct thinking during stressful times. Joshua was leading a huge company of Israelites into the Promised Land after having wandered in the wilderness for forty years. Talk about stress! But God's instructions to Joshua were, *"Have I not commanded you? Be strong and of good courage; do not be afraid, nor be dismayed, for the Lord your God is with you wherever you go,"* (Joshua 1:9). Science has shown us that the emotion of courage keeps our blood vessels from constricting during times of stress, preventing the harmful effects of stress on our body.

ACT: When we choose to connect with others we can create stress resilience. The harmful effects of stress are not inevitable. The stress hormone oxytocin can help us to strengthen our social connections and keep our body relaxed. Jesus had been preaching all day to a crowd of five thousand men, plus women and children. He must have been completely exhausted from a physical standpoint. But what did He do? He told the disciples to have everyone sit down and He fed them. He reached out to socially connect with all those people by providing a meal for them. However, what did He do after that? He sent the disciples away and reached out to His heavenly Father, connecting with Him through prayer. Spiritual connection with God is as important as social connection with others in order to build stress resilience.

RELAXATION TECHNIQUES

If we want to conquer brain strain, it is essential to master some relaxation techniques. These techniques are powerful tools to activate the relaxation response in our body. The relaxation response is a physical state of deep rest that changes our response to stress both physically and emotionally. There are many examples of relaxation techniques, but the goal of all of them is to cut off the cortisol surge from our adrenal glands during times of chronic stress in order to give our body time to recover. Some common examples include:

Relaxation Breathing: slow, focused diaphragmatic breathing.

Simply inhale slowly to the count of five through your nose while allowing your belly to expand. It may help to place one hand on your chest and the other on your belly to ensure that you are not doing "chest breathing." The hand on your chest should remain still while the hand on your belly rises with your inhalation. Hold your breath for the count of five and then slowly exhale through your mouth with pursed lips such as when you are blowing out a candle. Continue this slow, rhythmic breathing for about five minutes (shorter if time is limited) and allow your body to completely relax. Research from Harvard University by Dr. Herbert Benson clearly demonstrated how relaxation breathing can immediately regulate the HPA axis and turn off the cortisol surge. I have often personally used this technique very effectively to immediately relax when involved in particularly stressful situations. Hint: If you're out in public, use the restroom to do some relaxation breathing and you will be surprised at the positive effect on your mind and body.

Progressive Muscle Relaxation: tensing and then relaxing every muscle in your body from your forehead to your feet and toes.

This technique will help you to create awareness of tension and relaxation as it proceeds through all the major muscle groups, tensing and then relaxing them one at a time. The goal is to achieve total muscle relaxation. With ongoing practice you will reap the benefits and feel refreshed, calm, and relaxed after this activity. Tense each muscle group for about five seconds and then RELAX. Here's how to do it.

- Forehead: Wrinkle your forehead and try to make your eyebrows reach your hairline. Hold for five seconds and then relax.
- Eyes and nose: Close your eyes as tightly as you can for five seconds and then relax.
- Lips, cheeks, and jaw: Grimace for about five seconds and tightly purse your lips. Then relax, allowing your jaw to comfortably drop.
- Hands: Extend your hands in front of you. Clench your fists for five seconds and then relax. Then spread your fingers as far as they will go. Hold for five seconds and then relax.
- Forearms: Extend your arms forward as if to push against an invisible wall. Push for about five seconds and then relax.
- Upper arms: Bend at the elbows and tense your biceps as if

lifting a weight. Hold for about five seconds and then relax.

- Shoulders: Shrug your shoulders up towards your ears and hold for five seconds. Then relax.
- Back: Lie on the floor and arch your back. Hold for five seconds and then relax.
- Stomach: Tighten your stomach muscles for five seconds and then relax.
- Hips and buttocks: Squeeze your buttock muscles and hips. Hold for five seconds and then relax.
- Thighs: Press your legs together as tightly as you can for five seconds. Then relax.
- Feet: Bend your ankles toward your body as far as you can and hold for five seconds. Then relax. Repeat by bending your ankles away from your body as far as you can and hold for five seconds. Then relax.
- Toes: Curl your toes as tightly as you can for five seconds. Then relax. Repeat by spreading your toes as wide as possible. Hold for five seconds and then relax.

Focus on the feeling of relaxation and focus on any muscles that may still feel tense. The more you practice this activity, the more your relaxation will increase.

Imagery: activating your five senses as you focus on a place which is relaxing for you.

Sit comfortably in a chair with both feet on the floor. Alternately, you may choose to lie down on your back. Close your eyes and take two or three relaxation breaths described above. As you continue to breathe, allow your mind to take you to a place which is particularly relaxing for you. It may be the beach with the warm sand under your feet, the sound of the crashing waves, the smell of the salt air, and the breeze in your hair. Or it may be a scenic and tranquil mountain trail, the smell of pine trees and their soft needles under foot, a crystal clear mountain lake on which to kayak as you reach over and feel the cool water. The more you engage all your five senses in this exercise, the greater the relaxation you will experience. See, hear, touch, smell, and even taste—if your relaxing experience is enjoying a good meal at a fine restaurant. Finish your imagery by doing two to three minutes of relaxation breathing and slowly reorient to your surroundings.

Mindfulness: staying in the present or paying attention to your present experience, both external and internal.

Mindfulness means focusing on the sensations of our body, being aware of our thoughts and emotions, or simply noticing the world around us. It is about quieting a busy mind and being more aware of the present. What do you see? What do you hear? What do you smell? Are you sitting or standing? Is the surface hard or soft? Are you comfortable or uncomfortable? If you are eating, what does the food taste like—salty, sweet, pungent, or chewy? This technique is especially important to learn if you are suffering from anxiety or depression. The past is finished. There are no "do-overs." The future is yet to occur. Simply notice the present with curiosity and without judgment. Multi-tasking and the technology available today have influenced us to fracture our attention into smaller and smaller bits. We feel constantly distracted. While at our child's swim meet or soccer game we may hear the familiar "bing" from our phone or tablet and find ourselves checking emails from work and responding to a colleague's concern rather than being totally present at the event. Or worse, we may be posting or responding to posts on Facebook or other social media. According to Business Insider, Americans spend an average of 37 minutes daily on social media, a higher amount of time than on any other major Internet activity, including email. More than half of that time is spent not on desktop computers, but on smartphones and tablets. The Austrian psychiatrist, Viktor Frankl says, **"Between stimulus and response there is a space. In that space is our power to choose our response. In our response lies our growth and our freedom."** What response will you choose?

The Bible tells us in James 1:5-6 *"If any of you lacks wisdom, let him ask of God, who gives to all liberally and without reproach, and it will be given to him. But let him ask in faith, with no doubting, for he who doubts is like a wave of the sea driven and tossed by the wind."* Do you sometimes feel driven and tossed by anxious thoughts? Quieting your mind spiritually is a very important part of the relaxation response and mindfulness training. The Bible has much to say about our minds and meditation. Isaiah 40:31 says, *"But those who wait on the Lord shall renew their strength; they shall mount up with wings like eagles, they shall run and not be weary, they shall walk and not faint."* Notice that the passage doesn't say that the cause of the stress will disappear, but rather that our strength will be renewed. We will be able to soar above our circumstances and not be weary!

The Bible recounts a number of examples of meditation. Genesis 24:63 tells us that Isaac went out into the field to meditate. Joshua commanded the children of Israel to meditate in the Book of the Law day and night (Joshua 1:8). In the book of Psalms, David mentions three things upon which he meditated: the word of God or law of the Lord, including His precepts and statutes; God's wonderful works and deeds; and God Himself and *"the glorious splendor of His majesty"* (Psalm 1:2, 63:6, 77:12, 119:15, 23, 27, 48, 78, 148, 143:5, 145:5). Psalm 4:4 says, *"Meditate within your heart on your bed, and be still."* David also relates the fact that while lying in bed he calls to remembrance songs in the night, (Psalm 77:6). Sounds like a good cure for insomnia! A final passage in Isaiah 26:3 gives us a promise from God that says, *"You will keep him in perfect peace, whose mind is stayed on You, because he trusts in You."* Why not give mindfulness a try as a relaxation technique?

Practice for 10 to 15 minutes at least twice daily keeping your mind in the present. Begin by closing your eyes and taking some relaxation breaths to help quiet your mind. Don't worry if your mind seems to wander. Just breathe in and out for several minutes. Notice the sounds that you hear, the texture of the surface where you are sitting or lying, and any smells that you might notice. As you focus on your surroundings and continue to breathe in and out, your senses become more exquisite and fine-tuned, giving you a better appreciation for the present. When you are ready, begin focusing on our awesome, all-powerful God. No matter what you may be encountering in your life, God's attributes are limitless and beyond understanding. Job 26:14 says, *"Indeed these are the mere edges of His ways, and how small a whisper we hear of Him! But the thunder of His power who can understand?"*

Here are some of God's attributes on which to meditate:

Almighty, All-Knowing, Bountiful, Compassionate, Dependable, Disciplinarian, Eternal, Ever-Present, Faithful, Foreknowing, Forgiving, Generous, Giver of Good Gifts, Glorious, God of Gods, Good, Gracious, Great, Holy, Infinite, Impartial, Jealous, Joy, Just, Lawgiver, Listening, Longsuffering, Lord of Lords, Loving, Majestic, Merciful, Morally Perfect, Peace, Personal, Perfect Judge, Powerful, Promise-Keeper, Protector, Provider, Pure, Redeemer, Righteous, Self-Existent, Sovereign, Teacher, Transcendent, Trustworthy, Truth, Unchanging, Wise.

Select one or two attributes and focus your thoughts on these. Psalm 46: 10 says, *"Be still, and know that I am God; I will be exalted among the nations, I will be exalted in the earth!"* Other mindfulness techniques include reading or reciting from memory a favorite Bible passage, Psalm, or other inspirational poetry. Reading, listening to, or singing hymns can also help to bring your brain into balance. If you don't have a hymn book, get one. It doesn't matter if you are musical or not. Read the words and really meditate on the truths being expressed. You will find your spirit renewed and your circumstances put into perspective.

Anything that breaks the train of everyday thought can promote the relaxation response. Find what works for you and practice it for ten to twenty minutes twice a day. A repetitive sport such as running, stretching exercises, knitting, crocheting, or playing a musical instrument can all help us to let go of tension. Science has demonstrated that the relaxation response is so powerful because it lowers our blood pressure, heart rate, and the amount of oxygen our body consumes. Research has also demonstrated that practicing the relaxation response can help to alleviate symptoms associated with arthritis, insomnia, anxiety, depression, and cancer. **The operative word is "practice."** While our hands are repetitively looping the yarn and moving the knitting or crocheting needles, focus on slowly and rhythmically breathing in and out to the count of five. As we mow the lawn, tighten and relax every set of muscles in our body, including our face, neck, shoulders, arms, hands, back, stomach, buttocks, legs, and feet. For those of us who have placed our faith in the Lord Jesus Christ, follow the instructions found in Colossians 3: 2-3: *"Set your mind on things above, not on things on the earth. For you died, and your life is hidden with Christ in God."* The mind is an incredible organ. Inducing the relaxation response will help us to feel more in control, refreshed, improve our concentration, energy level, and self-acceptance. Most importantly, it will give us a sense of inner peace as our body becomes less responsive to the stress hormones.

COGNITIVE RESTRUCTURING

Cognitive restructuring is another important strategy for addressing brain strain. Cognitive distortions are the ways that our minds convince us of something that isn't really true. They are inaccurate thoughts that reinforce negative thinking or emotions. There are ten basic cognitive distortions. We need to get acquainted with each one and ask ourselves if any of them apply to us.

All-or-nothing thinking: All-or-nothing thinking looks at everything as completely black or white with no middle ground. It is often bound up with perfectionism. This type of thinking says things like, "If I fall short of perfection, I'm a total failure." How does perfectionism play out in your life? Does it keep you from showing hospitality to others? Or even worse, does it keep you from interacting socially with others for fear of not being "good enough?"

Mental filter: The mental filter focuses on the negatives while filtering out the positives. This thinking notices the one thing that went wrong rather than all the things that went right.

Overgeneralization: This type of thinking sees a single negative event as a never-ending pattern of defeat. It is closely linked to the fourth cognitive distortion, disqualifying the positive.

Disqualifying the positive: In this type of thinking we insist that positive experiences "don't count" for some reason or another. For example, we might think, "I did well on this exam, but that was just luck." We maintain a negative belief that our experience contradicts.

Jumping to conclusions: This distortion assumes a negative interpretation even though there are no definite facts supporting our conclusions. Two types of thinking associated with this distortion are "mind reading" and "fortune-telling." Have you ever found yourself concluding that someone is reacting negatively toward you without checking it out—" I can tell she secretly hates me." Or perhaps we simply anticipate that something will turn out badly based on our own prediction—" I just know something terrible is going to happen."

Catastrophizing: In this type of thinking we expect the worst case scenario to happen or exaggerate the importance of something—such as our "goof-up" or someone else's achievement.

Emotional reasoning: Emotional reasoning assumes that our negative emotions and feelings must reflect the way things really are. "Because I feel frightened right now, that must mean I'm an incompetent mother."

Should statements: "Musts" and "oughts" are in this same category. This type of thinking holds us to a strict list of what we should and shouldn't do, such as beating ourselves up if we break any of the rules. These feelings often lead to guilt. If we direct "should statements" toward others, we may feel anger, frustration, and resentment.

Labeling and mislabeling: This type of thinking is an extreme form of over-generalization in which we label ourselves based on mistakes and perceived shortcomings. "I'm a failure, an idiot, a loser." Mislabeling involves describing an event with language that is highly colored and emotionally loaded.

Personalization: This type of distortion occurs when we assume responsibility for things outside of our control. "It's my fault that my son got in an accident. I should have warned him to drive carefully in the rain."

HORMONES & BRAIN STRAIN—IS YOUR BRAIN HEADED FOR TROUBLE?

The brain has an elaborate warning system to let us know that it is headed for trouble. This may include physical ailments like headaches, fatigue, digestive problems, or insomnia. Emotional symptoms may also surface such as anxiety, difficulty concentrating, and feeling overwhelmed. Does any of this sound familiar? Brain strain is a huge problem today, especially for women in our supercharged, hyperlinked, productivity-consumed world of smart-phones, tablets, and laptops. Our brain is being asked to mobilize and maintain a state of high alertness for long hours every day. In addition, women often have the added responsibility of juggling work, children, and household needs. Premenstrual, pregnancy, postpartum, perimenopausal, and menopausal hormonal events can tip the balance, causing symptoms of depression and anxiety.

The combination of daily life and hormonal life may constitute a biochemical challenge to a woman's brain, a perfect example of brain strain or allostatic loading. This hyper-alert state leads to chronic brain dysregulation. People often feel that they need antidepressants merely to go on with their lives. The brain is not equipped to handle the battering impact of modern culture and antidepressants often serve as brain-stress stabilizers. In fact, more than one in ten Americans ages twelve and older report taking an antidepressant medication according to the Centers for Disease Control. Antidepressants are the most commonly prescribed medications second only to drugs that lower cholesterol!

A woman's unique reproductive cycle in and of itself has the capacity to destabilize the delicate balance of brain chemistry as much as stressful situations do. Hormonal events are powerful enough on their own to thrust the brain biochemistry into dysregulation. If a woman has a family history of mood disturbances, she may experience her first inkling of depression in the premenstrual period. Women with either Premenstrual Syndrome (PMS) or Premenstrual Dysphoric Disorder (PMDD) symptoms are more prone to serious mood disturbances later in their lives. Because our emotions and moods are influenced by such a complex variety of circumstances—hormonal, emotional, environmental, and spiritual, it is important that we track and understand the factors that are contributing to our overall emotional health. Our emotions cannot be looked at in a vacuum. We need to be able to track what is occurring in all aspects of our life to determine what is tipping the balance and causing our brain's self-regulatory systems to no longer be able to adapt to the increased demands. For an easy tool to help with mood monitoring, visit *www.YourMindRedefined.com* and download our Mood & Symptom Tracker. Don't let brain strain send you running for an anti-depressant or other medication before attempting to unravel the mystery of your emotions.

HORMONES: THE FUEL FOR HEALTH

"A period is just the beginning of a lifelong sentence."
-Cathy Crimmins

Hormones supervise the function of every cell in our body. They are chemical messengers that coordinate complex processes like growth, metabolism, and fertility. They can also influence the immune system and even alter behavior. Hormones guide social and sexual interactions as well as aggressive behaviors. They can influence worrying about hurting other's feelings, being optimistic or pessimistic, joyful or tearful, or experiencing self-doubt or self-confidence. Declining hormone levels have a straight line correlation with chronic, debilitating diseases such as arthritis, osteoporosis, mental decline, cancer, heart disease, obesity, loss of sex drive, incontinence, and many other problems. Therefore, hormones are needed as the fuel for health.

Various glands throughout the body produce, store, and secrete hormones into the bloodstream. These glands comprise the endocrine system. Endocrine actually means secreting internally. The most familiar endocrine glands are the ovaries and the testes also known as the gonads. In males, the testes produce sperm and secrete the male sex hormone testosterone; in females, the ovaries produce eggs and the female hormones estrogen and progesterone. The sex hormones determine secondary sex characteristics and also oversee sperm production, menstruation and pregnancy. The thyroid, pancreas, and adrenals are also endocrine glands which promote growth, metabolism, and the "fight or flight" response to stress. Hormones only influence the hormone's target cells which contain specific receptors to respond to the hormone. The hormone binds to the receptor and a response occurs. God designed and organized our brain's biochemistry to be highly receptive to hormones. A woman's brain carries countless receptor sites for the female sex hormones estrogen and progesterone, where they can fasten and exert their effects. A woman's reality can radically change from week to week based on hormonal changes not only throughout her menstrual cycle but throughout various stages of her life as well. Over the long haul, the brain mobilizes all the hormone systems to help a woman cope with financial problems, a poor marriage, social isolation, chronic low self-esteem, caring for sick family members, and so on. These stressful situations along with the emotions that accompany them result in a significant effect on stress pathways in the brain. It loads the brain's self-regulatory systems and eventually depletes or dysregulates the brain's coping mechanisms. Regardless of where we fall on the life continuum, from adolescence to post-menopausal, our hormones are impacting our brain and ultimately our mood. From the moment our ovaries spring into action, an orchestra begins to play in our brain—and the piece of music may be a beautiful symphony or it may become horribly discordant and out of tune.

Similar to women, male hormones determine what the brain is interested in doing. Their purpose, according to Dr. Loanne Brizendine MD, in her book The Male Brain, is to "help guide social, sexual, mating, parenting, protective, and aggressive behaviors." Research has shown that when a young man reaches puberty, testosterone increases twenty-fold along with an increase in brain circuitry for visual sex attraction. Then during fatherhood, testosterone actually decreases and the hormone prolactin increases allowing the father to be more attuned to hearing his baby cry. During a man's mid-life and into the andropause period – male menopause- testosterone very gradually decreases. This process is vastly different from female menopause which can result in a 75% decrease of progesterone by her mid-forties. For men, by age eighty-five, testosterone is about half of what it was at age twenty, yet a man can continue to reproduce during this time. What changes is that the ratio of estrogen to testosterone increases and oxytocin also increases. This increase in oxytocin makes a man more open to sentiment and affection with a focus on staying healthy, improving well-being, marriage, sex life, and relationships with his grandchildren. So you can see that hormones truly are the fuel for health.

As men age they are more prone to mood swings due to the decrease in testosterone levels. Mild mood swings in aging men due to low testosterone levels are normal. However, if a man has severe mood swings, especially if he is under thirty years old, it may be due to an underlying mental health disorder such as depression or bipolar disorder. Even though women are more prone to depression, men are not excluded from getting it. Men should seek a mental health professional for treatment if they believe that their mood swings are attributed to something other than aging.

The National Comorbidity Survey of 8,098 United States residents showed that women are approximately 1.7 times more likely than men to report a history of a major depressive episode. The difference in prevalence between genders begins in early adolescence and persists until women are in their mid-fifties. As estrogen levels vary throughout the lifespan, risk of depression in women also varies, and not all treatments are appropriate or effective at all times. A more recent population-based study with 3,481 participants demonstrated that women not only showed a higher risk for the onset of depression, but also experienced episodes that lasted approximately twenty weeks longer and tended to have a higher risk of depression reoccurring.

Women also are at higher risk for depression at specific points in their life when reproductive hormones fluctuate: in puberty, when estrogen is first rising; in the premenstrual phase; in pregnancy or the postpartum period; in association with infertility, miscarriage, or perinatal loss; and in the perimenopausal period. The only time that men and women are "equal" for risk of experiencing depressive episodes is prior to puberty and in older age after women have experienced menopause.

FEMALE ADOLESCENCE

During adolescence, huge surges of estrogen and progesterone begin pumping out, causing increased emotional impulses from the amygdala, the feeling part of the brain. However, the prefrontal cortex or the thinking part of the brain is not mature enough to handle these blasts of emotion. It has sprouted additional neurons, but the connections are thin and immature. Adolescents often do not consider the consequences of their behaviors. As a result, teenage girls often have frequent mood changes, becoming overwhelmed, impulsive, and often resentful of authorities who are seeking to "bolster the prefrontal cortex" and set limits. In addition, in the fourth week of a girl's menstrual cycle, the hormones bottom out precipitously and the brain becomes irritated because it is looking for their calming effect.

Another important hormone for teenage girls is oxytocin, the hormone of bonding. Relationships become very important. When a relationship is threatened or lost, the bottom drops out of the level of some of the female brain's neurochemicals such as serotonin, dopamine, and oxytocin, and the stress hormone cortisol take over. This change in neurochemicals and hormones often result in the girl becoming anxious and fearful of being rejected and left alone. She looks for the closeness of social connection and the good intimacy "drug" oxytocin. When there is social contact, there is a flood of oxytocin. If social contact is gone, oxytocin and dopamine bottom out, resulting in emotional trouble.

The first episodes of depression experienced by some females can coincide with puberty, though these episodes are often unrecognized by family members and untreated by clinicians. Some signs and symptoms of depression in adolescence include: no motivation and even becoming withdrawn, closing their bedroom door after school and staying in their room for hours, sleeping excessively, changing eating habits, DUI (Driving Under the Influence), shoplifting, complaints of pains, including headaches, stomachaches, low back pain, or fatigue, and rebelliousness . When the havoc of hormones is added to the many other changes happening in a teen's life, it's easy to see why their moods swing like a pendulum. If friends, family or things that a teen usually enjoys don't help to improve her sadness or sense of isolation, there's a good chance that she has depression. If a teen remains unhappy for more than two weeks, she probably needs treatment.

Adolescents and those under twenty-five years old should only be treated with antidepressants after the risk and benefits have been carefully considered. Treatment with antidepressants in adolescents has become increasingly difficult due to the documented increased risk of suicide. In addition, there is limited documentation about the effectiveness of many antidepressants in adolescents less than eighteen years of age. The American Academy of Child and Adolescent Psychiatry recommends psychotherapy as the first line of treatment for adolescent depression and recommends reserving antidepressants for those with severe depression. In such cases, fluoxetine (Prozac) and escitalopram (Lexapro) are the only two antidepressants with documented efficacy and Food and Drug Administration (FDA) approval for use in adolescents. Prozac is approved for ages 8 and older; Lexapro for kids 12 and older. The FDA requires that all antidepressants include a "black box warning" about the increased risks of suicidal thinking and behavior in children, adolescents and young adults up to age 24. It is important to remember that antidepressants are used to treat the illness, not the behavior associated with it. The use of any medications should be coupled with careful monitoring and psychotherapy such as Cognitive Behavioral Therapy.

MENSTRUAL MOODS

During the fertility years, estrogen and progesterone follow a predictable path during each monthly cycle. There are repeated surges of estrogen and progesterone throughout the month, with surges varying from day-to-day and week-to-week. This fluctuation in estrogen and progesterone particularly affects the limbic system, or the feeling part of the brain.

Critical thinking may be sharpened at times and emotional responsiveness fine-tuned based on the levels of these hormones.

Estrogen is essential to keeping our brain functioning at an optimal level. It increases blood flow to the brain, decreases inflammation, and influences brain neurons and brain tissue. Estrogen also maintains the orderly firing rates of serotonin, dopamine, acetylcholine, and norepinephrine (NE), chemical messengers in the brain. This promotes positive moods, clear thinking and memory, motivation, sex drive, and stress responses. Estrogen contributes to a positive mood by increasing the amount of serotonin available in the synaptic space between neurons. Because of this action, some researchers have determined that estrogen is possibly a natural antidepressant and mood stabilizer.

Estrogen protects many aspects of brain functioning, particularly memory. It strongly enhances glutamate a neurotransmitter or chemical messenger that speeds up nerve communication in the brain which encourages mood stability. It also promotes the growth of nerve cells containing acetylcholine (ACH), particularly in the hippocampus. Memory function is dependent on adequate acetylcholine which promotes mental sharpness, sustains memory, and increases connections with other nerve cells. This function of estrogen helps to explain why Estrogen Replacement Therapy (ERT) in menopausal women helps to prevent memory difficulties and promotes word retrieval skills. Estrogen also protects neurons from environmental injury due to free radicals, lack of oxygen, and low blood sugar and protects neurons from damage by amyloid protein, which is implicated in the development of Alzheimer's disease.

Estrogen also affects the levels of serotonin, dopamine, norepinephrine, and acetylcholine, the neurotransmitters that control mood and memory. It increases their concentration by affecting their release, reuptake, and whether or not they are activated. Estrogen also increases the number of receptors for these neurotransmitters. In addition, estrogen influences the brain's blood supply. It binds to receptors in the lining of your blood vessels, and stimulates the release of nitric oxide, which causes our blood vessels to dilate. Estrogen also influences the blood supply to your brain by acting as an anti-inflammatory agent at the blood vessel wall, protecting it from damage by cytokines and free radicals and slowing down plaque formation.

Progesterone's name tells us its function: "pro"— for and "gest"— gestation. The major role of progesterone is to give a woman the ability to conceive and sustain pregnancy. It maintains the lining of the uterus from which the embryo receives sustenance during the first weeks of growth. There is a surge of progesterone at the time of ovulation which increases sex drive and the urge to procreate. Isn't it amazing how God intricately designed our bodies to link this hormonal surge to coincide with a woman's peak of fertility? Progesterone works in tandem with estrogen. If estrogen rises, we need progesterone to help balance estrogen. Progesterone decreases the number of available estrogen receptors which may be one of the mechanisms by which it can induce depression. There is evidence that at the end of the menstrual cycle, progesterone can actually dismantle the nerve connections that estrogen established at the beginning

A woman has very little progesterone until she starts ovulating. The body never overproduces it; however, during pregnancy a large amount of it is manufactured to support the developing fetus. There is barely any progesterone during the first two weeks of a monthly cycle. After ovulation, at around day fourteen, it begins to build, reaching peak levels at about day twenty-one. If no fertilization occurs, the body pulls the switch and the hormone level starts falling. The progesterone phase is very precise and lasts for two weeks after ovulation.

Progesterone is important for many reasons other than maintaining a pregnancy. According to Dr. John Lee MD, a pioneer in women's health and bio-identical hormones, the following are some of the intrinsic effects of progesterone:

- Mild diuretic
- Helps use fat for energy
- Natural antidepressant
- Helps thyroid hormone action
- Normalizes blood clotting
- Maintains proper cell oxygen levels
- Protects against breast cysts
- Protects against breast cancer
- Protects against endometrial cancer
- Moisturizes skin when used topically
- Counteracts estrogen side effects

It is important to note that progesterone is the precursor to all the other sex hormones including estrogen, the corticosteroids - essential for the stress response, sugar, electrolyte balance, and blood pressure. (See Appendix II: Steroid Hormone Cascade) Since progesterone is a precursor to so many other hormones, it is easy to see why a deficiency in progesterone can cause a wide range of problems. In a landmark study at the Mayo Clinic, the beneficial effect of progesterone compared to non-bioidentical progestin included a 30% reduction in sleep problems, a 50% reduction in anxiety, a 60% reduction in depression, a 25% reduction in menstrual bleeding, a 40% reduction in cognitive difficulties, and a 30% improvement in sexual function. Eighty percent of women in the study reported overall satisfaction with the bio-identical progesterone formulation. Symptoms of progesterone deficiency include getting your first period relatively late, a history of infrequent periods with minor bleeding - oligomenorrhea or amenorrhea - no period at all, heavy and frequent periods possibly due to tissue building up in the uterus, spotting a few days before your period due to progesterone dropping prematurely in your cycle, difficulty becoming pregnant, and difficulty carrying to term.

Estrogen and progesterone surges primarily affect the hippocampus where emotions and memories are connected by changing a woman's sensitivity to stress from week to week. These fluctuations will continue until the woman passes through menopause. Estrogen acts like a "fertilizer" for the brain cells, making a woman more socially relaxed during the first two weeks. In fact, there is a 25% growth of connections in the hippocampus which makes the brain a little bit sharper. When ovulation occurs, halfway through the 28-day cycle, progesterone rises and reverses the actions of estrogen in the hippocampus. The brain becomes more sedated, sometimes irritable, and less focused. In the last few days of her cycle when progesterone collapses, the calming effect is abruptly withdrawn and many teenage girls and women find themselves screaming, or crying over silly sentimental things like hearing a song on the radio, or even a commercial on TV. Some women who are particularly sensitive to these hormonal fluctuations start behaving erratically at home, work, and school. This behavior is referred to as Premenstrual Syndrome (PMS) or in its more severe presentation involving a predominance of mood symptoms, Premenstrual Dysphoric Disorder (PMDD).

Approximately 75% of women experience a premenstrual change with emotional, physical, or behavioral symptoms commonly referred to as premenstrual syndrome or PMS. For most women, the symptoms are mild and tolerable. However, 3% – 9% experience moderate to severe premenstrual mood symptoms which can be disabling and may cause significant disruption in their lives. This disorder is known as Premenstrual Dysphoric Disorder or PMDD. The most common symptom is irritability; however, other symptoms may include a depressed mood, anxiety, or mood swings. A distinguishing characteristic of both PMS and PMDD is the timing of symptom onset. In women with both PMS and PMDD, mood symptoms occur only during the luteal phase of the menstrual cycle - ovulation until onset of menses - and resolve after menstruation onset. During the follicular phase of the menstrual cycle - the first day of the menstrual cycle until ovulation - a woman's moods and her level of functioning return back to normal. Females whose ovaries make the most estrogen and progesterone are the most resistant to stress because they have more serotonin cells in their brains helping them to feel at ease. Women with the least estrogen and progesterone are more sensitive to stress and have fewer serotonin brain cells. For women who are the most stress-sensitive, the final days before their periods can become a living nightmare.

Premenstrual symptoms can be physical, emotional, or behavioral. Physical symptoms can include: headaches, migraines, breast tenderness, abdominal cramps, bloating, weight gain, skin changes, acne, hot flashes, diarrhea, constipation, general malaise, nausea, lack of appetite, palpitations, and fatigue. Emotional symptoms can include: irritability, depression, tearfulness, anxiety, nervousness, mood changeability, sadness, anger, rage, hostility, oversensitivity, easily overwhelmed, "raw" feelings, tremulousness, and jumpiness. Behavioral symptoms can include: food cravings, decreased interest in activities, work, relationships, social isolation, avoidance of activities, poor concentration, clumsiness, decreased libido, slower, muddled thinking, increase in alcohol consumption, increased food binging, and perception problems.

PMS and PMDD criteria share symptoms. However, PMDD requires greater than or equal to five symptoms almost every month during the luteal phase, with greater than or equal to one mood symptom such as depression, anxiety, irritability, etc. The mood symptoms must predominate over the somatic complaints such as headaches, breast tenderness, and abdominal cramps. PMDD also has greater functional impairment, meaning that the symptoms interfere with work, school, social activities, or relationships. In order to make the diagnosis, these symptoms must be confirmed by prospective daily ratings for at least two consecutive cycles in which you are experiencing symptoms. Using a monthly chart can be therapeutic in and of itself by helping identify the relationship between your monthly cycle and mood changes. It may also help you to anticipate the days that you may be at risk for mood worsening. Log onto *www.YourMindRedefined.com* where you can download our Mood & Symptom Tracker form. Use this form to record your symptoms for two consecutive months and bring your results to discuss treatment options with your healthcare provider. There is definitely hope and treatment.

NON-PHARMACOLOGIC TREATMENT

Lifestyle changes can help to alleviate mild symptoms. While there is no solid research evidence, decreasing caffeine, sugar, and sodium can be helpful. In addition, decrease your alcohol and nicotine use as well as ensure that you get adequate sleep. For a complete discussion about sleep strategies, see the chapter on "Use Your Brain to Overcome Insomnia."

Certain nutritional supplements have been shown to improve symptoms. Of particular note was a large multicenter study which showed that 1200 mg. of calcium per day significantly reduced both the physical and emotional symptoms of PMS. Vitamin B_6 50 to 100 mg. per day can also have beneficial effects; however, do not take over 100 mg. per day as this can cause peripheral neuropathy (weakness, numbness/tingling, or burning/stabbing pain in hands or feet). There is also limited evidence that magnesium (200 – 360 mg. per day) and Vitamin E (400 IU per day) can also provide some relief of symptoms.

A recent double-blind, placebo-controlled study on 178 women who met the criteria for PMS demonstrated that one tab per day of the herb Chasteberry (agnus castus fruit extract) significantly decreased symptoms of irritability, anger, headache, and breast fullness compared with placebo. Bloating was unaffected, however. The effects of the plant seem to work by increasing the production of progesterone by mimicking the corpus luteum and stimulating the production of lutenizing hormone. Another study found that gingko biloba improved symptoms of breast tenderness and fluid retention. A review of studies about evening primrose oil, however, found that it was no more effective than placebo in treating PMS symptoms. Light therapy is also being explored as a possible treatment for PMDD. Finally, Cognitive Behavioral Therapy (CBT) has been demonstrated to be an effective non-pharmacological approach for the treatment of PMS and PMDD. Research has shown that CBT was as effective as fluoxetine (Prozac) 20 mg. daily in the treatment of PMDD.

PHARMACOLOGIC TREATMENT

Psychotropic Medications

Selective serotonin reuptake inhibitors (SSRIs) are the first-line of treatment for premenstrual mood symptoms. There is significant research supporting the effectiveness of SSRIs in reducing both the emotional and physical symptoms of PMS and PMDD. Most women respond to a low dose and the response occurs in only a few days rather than the two to three week response time when treating depression. Some women take their medication only during the last two weeks of their menstrual cycle while others take the medication continuously. New studies have also begun to examine whether some women can take the medication only at the onset of their symptoms and still get a positive response. Other types of antidepressants which block the reabsorption (reuptake) of the neurotransmitter serotonin in the brain have also been shown to be helpful in treating premenstrual symptoms. These include clomipramine (Anafranil) which is a tricyclic antidepressant, venlafaxine (Effexor), and duloxetine (Cymbalta) which are serotonin and norepinephrine reuptake inhibitors (SNRIs). Anxiety symptoms of PMS and PMDD are sometimes treated with a benzodiazepine such as alprazolam (Xanax). However, this medication should be used cautiously due to the potential for addiction.

Women, who have a diagnosis of premenstrual exacerbation of a mood disorder (PME), generally do not respond well to intermittent dosing of an antidepressant. Rather, raising the dose during the luteal phase of their cycle (during the last two weeks) and then returning to the lower dose when menses begins is a better option. Another option confirmed by research is to add oral contraceptives to their antidepressant therapy. If you have bipolar disorder and you experience premenstrual mood worsening, be aware that adding an antidepressant or increasing the dose puts you at risk for mania or hypomania.

Hormonal Interventions

Hormonal treatments of PMS or PMDD are based on preliminary research that suppression of ovulation eliminates premenstrual symptomatology. This theory was considered as early as the late 1880s by a physician named Charcot. Charcot viewed hysteria as an inherited disease which could be triggered by emotional or physical trauma and believed that there were definably pathophysiological pathways that could be activated by the physician under hypnosis. Seizures were considered the central sign of hysterical disorders. The treatment he prescribed was a device that he invented known as the ovary compressor. It was made of leather with metal screws affixed to it. The leather straps were fastened around the woman's back. The screws, which had leather padding, were placed over the abdomen and then slowly tightened causing the padding to squeeze the women's uterus. The belief was that if you could get the ovaries to calm down a woman would stop having these hysterical behaviors. What's interesting is that current research has demonstrated that ovulation suppression can stop PMDD. Oral birth control pills, particularly Yasmin (FDA approved in 2001) and Yaz (FDA approved in 2006), have been shown to be effective treatment for PMDD. Unfortunately, these newer oral contraceptives contain synthetic progesterone known as drospirenone which can cause elevated levels of potassium, low sodium, electrolyte imbalance, heart arrhythmias, heart attack, stroke, gall bladder problems, blood clots, embolisms, and sudden death. Women should discuss the risk and benefits of drospirenone-containing birth control pills with their health care provider, including the risk for developing blood clots before taking these hormones. The Food and Drug Administration states that although "the risk of blood clots is higher when using any birth control pills than not using them, it still remains lower than the risk of developing blood clots in pregnancy and in the postpartum period." However, if you have a history of blood clots, strokes, or migraines, you are thirty-five years of age or older, or you smoke, you should not use oral contraceptive pills.

MOMMY MOODS

Throughout pregnancy, a woman's brain is flooded in neurohormones manufactured by the fetus and placenta. Once your blood supply has joined with your developing baby, at about only two weeks after fertilization, the hormonal changes begin. Progesterone levels start to climb in both your bloodstream and brain. The purpose is to keep the pregnancy viable until the placenta takes over. The progesterone may also contribute to depression. In fact, it spikes from 10 to 100 times its normal level during the first two to four months of pregnancy. Its sedating effects are similar to the anti-anxiety medication, Valium. The brain becomes somewhat sedated and brain circuits become mellow. A woman needs to sleep and eat more. Thirst and hunger centers are switched on full blast by rising hormones. Also, the brain is changing how it reacts to certain smells. It becomes overly sensitive and protective. By the fourth month, the brain becomes accustomed to the massive hormone changes and becomes more focused on what is going on in our uterus. The receptors and pathways settle down, enjoying all the extra (antidepressant) estrogen that is circulating. This additional estrogen may contribute to feelings of euphoria. At the fifth month, an expectant mother begins to notice her baby's movements. She becomes consciously aware of her growing baby.

Estrogen levels rise rapidly in early weeks of pregnancy altering the functioning of the serotonin, dopamine, and norepinephrine pathways in the limbic system or feeling part of the brain. High estrogen levels along with the tranquilizing effect of high progesterone help protect against stress hormones during pregnancy. Regular hormonal cycles do not resume until after a woman stops nursing. Approximately 90% of postpartum depression episodes occur within the first four weeks after delivery.

Cortisol and other stress hormones are produced in large quantities by both the developing baby and the placenta resulting in the mother's body and brain being flooded with them. By late pregnancy, the stress hormone levels are as high as they would be during strenuous exercise—three times the normal amount! Even though elevated cortisol levels are often found in depressed patients, during pregnancy they don't result in the feeling of stress. Instead, they help a pregnant woman to remain vigilant about her safety, nutrition, and surroundings. Prolactin, the hormone responsible for milk production, also rises progressively throughout pregnancy. Elevated prolactin has been shown to be associated with irritability, and anger.

At the time of birth, estrogen stimulates the rise of oxytocin which causes the uterus to start contracting and aids the passage of milk down the milk ducts for breast-feeding. At the same time, the level of progesterone suddenly collapses. Oxytocin and dopamine work together to create a sense of euphoria or intense excitement and happiness as well as increase the senses of hearing, touch, sight, and smell. These surges of oxytocin and dopamine in the brain create the bond, switching off judgmental thinking and negative emotions and switching on pleasure circuits that create feelings of attachment. Dopamine is the pleasure and reward chemical. It is enhanced by the estrogen and oxytocin in the new mother's brain. The nurturing response of the oxytocin circuits are reinforced by the feeling of pleasure created by bursts of dopamine. This is the same reward circuit set off in a woman's brain by intimate communication and orgasm with her spouse. In fact, if you were to view this phenomenon on an MRI you would see that mother love and romantic love look surprisingly the same. Skin to skin contact with babies, including breastfeeding, reinforces this hardwired response of oxytocin and dopamine. Many of the positive feelings a woman usually gets from sexual intercourse, are evoked several times daily by meeting the physical needs of her children.

Breast-feeding can also heighten and prolong the mellow, mildly unfocused state that is pretty common after giving birth. Gloria, a patient of mine who was a highly educated woman, was stunned after giving birth that she had tremendous difficulty even summoning basic words and phrases needed to hold an intelligent conversation. She experienced an alarming level of mental fog. However, it soon passed after she weaned her son. Another contributing factor to this mental fog includes lack of sleep. **New mothers lose an average of 700 hours of sleep in the first year postpartum.** That's equivalent to twenty-nine days and four hours without sleep! Additionally, brain size actually shrinks during pregnancy and only returns to normal about 6 months postpartum.

Many mothers suffer "withdrawal" symptoms when they are separated physically from their babies. They develop feelings of fear, anxiety, waves of panic. These feelings are both a psychological state and a neurochemical state. Declining levels of the stress-regulating brain chemical oxytocin are thought to be the reason. Nursing mothers also go through withdrawal symptoms when they wean. This usually occurs in conjunction with returning to a stressful workplace which also can induce an anxious, agitated state. Oxytocin was flooding the mother's brain every few hours from nursing, and now the supply is cut-off. Oxytocin only lasts about one to three hours in the bloodstream and the brain, so the solution is fairly straightforward. The mother should pump breast milk at work as long as possible and slowly taper off breast feeding, continuing to nurse evenings and weekends. This allows her to still get the pleasurable oxytocin and dopamine boosts and to stay connected with her baby.

Postpartum mood disorders, often broadly referred to as postpartum depression is a term for the wide range and variety of emotions that a woman can experience after having a baby. It is the biggest complication of birth today, affecting at least one in ten women. According to Dr. Stahl in his book Stahl's Essential Psychopharmacology, women with a history of postpartum depression have a 63% risk of recurrence, whereas only one tenth of that risk exists if such patients take antidepressants. Also, women with any history of depression are twice as likely as never-depressed women to experience postpartum depression.

Postpartum mood disorders may represent a subset of women who are mood sensitive to hormonal fluctuations, similar to the issues with Premenstrual Dysphoric Disorder. Estrogen and progesterone are highest at the end of pregnancy. As soon as the placenta is delivered, the hormone levels drop precipitously. Amazingly, estrogen levels reach that of a normal menstrual cycle within 24 hours after delivery! There are numerous estrogen receptors in the limbic brain, and since this hormone contributes to mood stability, imagine how profoundly its rapid removal can impair mood health in vulnerable women! After the initial drop, estrogen levels remain somewhat low until the pituitary gland and ovaries resume the menstrual cycle. This amount of time can vary depending on whether or not the woman is breastfeeding. Hormones of lactation often suppress the pituitary from functioning and it may take months for the menstrual cycle to reestablish itself.

The new mother may experience a wide range of symptoms including depressive feelings, sadness, loss of interest and enjoyment in life, irritability, feeling overwhelmed, sleep and appetite disturbances, and altered or a negative self-view. Postpartum mood disorders are frequently characterized by a more anxious presentation. Symptoms include anxiety, racing thoughts, agitation, panic attacks, and even obsessions rather than a sad withdrawn demeanor. The symptoms generally impair the mother's ability to participate fully in life and the care of her newborn. There are three sub-categories to postpartum mood disorders:

Baby Blues

Baby Blues affects 50-80% of women postpartum. The new mother experiences feelings of being overwhelmed, crying frequently, mood swings with irritability and anxiousness, and sleep deprivation. It is a transitory condition which self-corrects in the first two to four weeks with support, sleep, and hormone stabilization. Sleep is especially important and whether or not a new mother is breastfeeding; she should be relieved of this responsibility at least one day per week by either pumping breast milk or supplementing with formula. Sleep deprivation can cause a new mother to easily progress from baby blues to postpartum depression.

Postpartum Depression

Postpartum Depression affects 10-20% of women postpartum.

Symptoms can occur soon after delivery or sometimes as late as one year postpartum. If your symptoms last longer than two weeks and do not resolve without treatment, you are probably suffering from postpartum depression. Some of the key symptoms include extreme fatigue, trouble sleeping and eating - even if support is available - no interest in the baby, withdrawing from family and friends, thoughts of hurting yourself or the baby, feeling sad, hopeless, overwhelmed, and guilty. In about 10% of women, symptoms may exhibit as anxiety and panic, obsessions and compulsions, or even Posttraumatic Stress (PTSD), particularly if there was real or perceived trauma during childbirth or immediately after the baby was born. PTSD symptoms affect about 1-6% of women. Unplanned cesarean births, emergency complications, or a baby having to stay in the Neonatal Intensive Care Unit (NICU), may all lead to PTSD symptoms. These symptoms include nightmares and flashbacks to the traumatic event, a feeling of detachment from reality and life, irritability, sleeplessness, hypervigilance, and being easily startled. Regardless of how it manifests, postpartum depression is a clinical condition that requires treatment, either with therapy, medications, or both. Two highly effective therapy approaches are cognitive behavioral therapy and interpersonal therapy. Some women develop very scary obsessional thoughts toward their new baby. These obsessions or thoughts are persistent, repetitive, and can include mental images of the baby that are disturbing. It is very important to tell someone you trust about your feelings and thoughts so that they can help you get the needed treatment.

Postpartum Psychosis

Postpartum psychosis affects one to three women in every thousand deliveries. This is a psychiatric emergency and can occur as early as 24 hours postpartum. It usually shows up within the first two to three weeks postpartum. The symptoms include a loss of touch with reality, bizarre behavior, extreme agitation, confusion, hallucinations, delusions, and inability to sleep, eat, or maintain a coherent conversation. Moods seesaw between euphoria and profound depression. The mother is often suicidal and frequently acts on it. She may harm or kill the infant as a result of delusional thinking. It is crucial that the mother and baby are kept safe. Hospitalization is almost always necessary to stabilize the mother.

The rapid drop in estrogen levels is strongly implicated as the trigger in women who are genetically vulnerable. It causes a sequence of biochemical events in numerous interacting pathways in the brain. It has been proposed that the dopamine receptors in the dopamine pathway are more sensitive in postpartum women who become psychotic. Rapid drop in estrogen may alter these receptors. Postpartum psychosis often occurs in women with Bipolar Disorder, a history of PMDD, mood swings from oral contraceptives, or mood destabilization from fertility drugs. **A high-risk woman must be sure to designate a trusted person to watch her carefully for any mood, thought, or behavior changes postpartum to be sure that she and the baby are kept safe and that she gets appropriate treatment.**

MENOPAUSAL MOODS

Menopause is defined as the permanent end of menstruation and fertility. It occurs twelve months after the last menstrual period. As a woman approaches her late thirties, her ovaries produce less estrogen and progesterone, the hormones that regulate menstruation, and her fertility begins to drop. This is the beginning of the time known as perimenopause when the "conversation" between the ovaries and the brain gradually slows down and can last anywhere from seven to ten years. The estrogen doesn't decline in a nice, smooth, orderly fashion, however. Instead, it is a jerky ride downhill. You can actually have dramatic hormone surges while your ovaries are transitioning to menopause—think of these as "sun flares," surges of hormones followed by "crashes." It's the ride from the surges to the crashes that can precipitate irritability, dysphoria, anxiety, and even panic.

Contrary to popular belief, hot flashes are not the most prevalent difficulty. Irritability, insomnia, and depressed mood rank among the most common complaints. If a woman complains of a loss of well-being, mild depressive symptoms, fatigue, and sleep disturbances, along with hot flashes and changes in her menstrual cycle, she may be in the perimenopause phase even if she is only in her thirties! As early as their mid-thirties, many women's progesterone levels have dropped to at least 50%! Reduction in progesterone is earlier and more rapid than the decline of estrogen which leaves the body vulnerable to estrogen dominance. Dietary and environmental issues compound the problem. Although both soy and dairy products contain progesterones, they also are high in xenoestrogens. Xenoestrogens are endocrine disrupters that mimic estrogen and block or bind to your hormone receptors, contributing to a situation known as estrogen dominance. If estrogen rises, you need progesterone to off-set it. The influence of estrogen-mimicking chemicals found in herbicides, pesticides, and petrochemicals like BPA and PCBs found in some cosmetics, glue, and plastics, as well as using an estrogen patch following a hysterectomy all contribute to estrogen dominance. Some of the symptoms that a woman may experience are: irregular periods, heavy bleeding and out of control cycles, food cravings, bloating, weight gain, fatigue, mood swings, depression, an impatient but clear mind, cyclical migraine headaches, lack of sexual desire, menstrual cramps, breast/nipple tenderness, breast fullness, and hair loss. Estrogen dominance is the root cause of problems such as endometriosis – the appearance of endometrial tissue outside the uterus and causing pelvic pain - fibroids, polyps, adenomyosis - when endometrial tissue which lines the uterus grows into the muscular wall of the uterus - irregular periods, fibrocystic breast disease, heavy bleeding, and breast, ovarian, and uterine cancer. In addition, as progesterone markedly decreases, there is frequently an insufficient amount to carry out the hormone's critical task of generating new bone tissue resulting in osteoporosis. Because of the rapid decline of progesterone compared to estrogen, all perimenopausal women are estrogen dominant and should consider adding some type of progesterone replacement to restore balance.

Unfortunately, a widespread misconception among healthcare providers is that progestins, such as Provera, are the same as bioidentical progesterone. This error has affected the health and well-being of millions of American women. Progestins are chemically synthesized from progesterone with a chemically altered structure. Progestins can bind to progesterone receptors within cells and therefore alter the action of the natural hormone. The Women's Health Initiative study in 2002 showed increased incidents of heart disease, breast cancer, and strokes among the women taking Premarin and Provera (PremPro) - synthetic progesterone. An alternative is Prometrium, the only bio-identical progesterone in pill form approved by the FDA and available through regular pharmacies in dosages of 100 and 200 milligrams.

However, according to Dr. Uzzi Reiss MD, an expert in the clinical application of bio-identical hormones, about 1/3 of his patients find that even the 100 milligram dose of Prometrium is too high. Natural progesterone capsules are available from a compounding pharmacy in four potencies: 25, 50, 75, and 100 milligrams, but the effectiveness of oral supplements may be limited due to the digestive process in the stomach. An alternative is bio-identical progesterone cream, gel, or sublingual drops. Most women over thirty-five can benefit from a daily dose of a non-prescription progesterone cream. Replacing progesterone is vital to maintain hormonal balance as well as to promote optimal health and wellness.

Dr. John Lee, a pioneer in the field of bio-identical hormones, identified twelve health benefits to maintaining adequate levels of progesterone.

1. Protects against breast fibrocysts
2. Promotes normal sleep patterns
3. Helps the body use fat for energy

4. Acts as a natural diuretic
5. Acts as a natural antidepressant and calms anxiety
6. Helps prevent cyclical migraines
7. Helps normalize blood sugar levels
8. Helps restore normal libido
9. Prevents endometrial and breast cancer
10. Stimulates new bone formation
11. Prevents autoimmune diseases
12. Improves the tone of our blood vessels

A pharmaceutical-grade 1.6% - 3% progesterone cream - about 450 - 500 mg. of progesterone per ounce - is the recommended strength. This concentration is very low and should not present any problems for most women. Always consult your healthcare provider before starting any type of hormone replacement. (See Appendix I for specific instructions about using progesterone cream).

On the other end of the spectrum, a number of organ systems are subject to deterioration over time without estrogen—our heart and blood vessels, vagina, lower urinary tract, bones, and brain.

Heart and blood vessel or cardiovascular disease

When our estrogen levels decline, our risk of cardiovascular disease increases. Heart disease is the leading cause of death in women and men. So it's important to get regular exercise, follow a Mediterranean diet, stop smoking, decrease our stress level, and maintain a normal weight. It is also important to take a medical-grade vitamin and mineral supplement which includes the nutrients for bone health, omega-3 fatty acids, vitamin B12 as a pre-metered spray for best absorption, vitamin D, and prebiotics and probiotics. You can check out these supplements and more in the chapter on "Diet, Exercise, & Supplements—The Sustainability of Health." Learn how to effectively manage your stress levels by reviewing the chapter on "How Brain Strain Sabotages Your Emotional Health—Is Your Brain on Strike?"

Osteoporosis

Osteoporosis causes bones to become porous, brittle, and weak, leading to an increased risk of fractures. Even bending over or coughing can cause a fracture to occur. Osteoporosis affects both men and women, but Caucasian and Asian women are at the greatest risk. The National Institutes of Health (NIH) list several risk factors that increase the chances of developing osteoporosis, including:

- a thin, small-boned frame

- previous fracture or family history of osteoporotic fracture
- estrogen deficiency resulting from early menopause before age 45, either naturally, from surgical removal of the ovaries, or as a result of prolonged amenorrhea - abnormal absence of menstruation - in younger women
- advanced age
- a diet low in calcium
- Caucasian and Asian ancestry (African American and Hispanic women are at lower but significant risk)
- cigarette smoking
- excessive use of alcohol
- prolonged use of certain medications.

According to the NIH, recent studies indicate a number of facts that highlight the risk that Asian American women face with regard to developing osteoporosis. Compared with Caucasian women, Asian women have been found to consume less calcium. One reason for this may be that up to ninety percent of Asian Americans are lactose intolerant. Therefore, they may avoid dairy products, the primary source of calcium in the diet. Calcium is essential for building and maintaining a healthy skeleton. Asian women generally have lower hip fracture rates than Caucasian women, although the prevalence of vertebral fractures among Asians seems to be as high as that in Caucasians. Slender women have less bone mass than heavy or obese women and, therefore, are at greater risk for osteoporotic bone fractures.

Most people reach their peak bone mass in their twenties. The greater our peak bone mass, the less likely we are to develop osteoporosis as we age. During the first few years after menopause, women often lose bone density at a rapid rate, increasing their risk of osteoporosis. The creation of new bone doesn't keep up with the removal of old bone. Postmenopausal women with osteoporosis are especially susceptible to fractures of their hips, wrists, and spine. There are at least twenty essential bone nutrients that we need to take daily to help maintain your bone health. Read about what they are and how they work in the chapter on "Diet, Exercise, & Supplements—What You Should Know." Weight-bearing exercises can also help to prevent bone loss and help to strengthen bones that are already weak. See your healthcare provider if you notice increased back pain which may be caused by a fractured or collapsed vertebra in your spine, loss of height (do your adult children keep asking you if you are getting shorter?), a stooped posture, or have a bone fracture more easily than expected—such as stepping off a curb or rolling over in bed.

Urinary incontinence

As our estrogen levels decrease, the tissues of the vagina and urethra lose their elasticity. We may experience a frequent, sudden, strong urge to urinate, followed by an involuntary loss of urine - urge incontinence - or the loss of urine with coughing, laughing or lifting - stress incontinence. We may also have urinary tract infections more often. Strengthening pelvic floor muscles with Kegel exercises and applying a topical vaginal estrogen may help relieve symptoms of incontinence.

Sexual function

Vaginal dryness from decreased moisture production and loss of elasticity can cause discomfort and slight bleeding during sexual intercourse. Also, decreased sensation may reduce the desire for sexual activity known as libido. Water-based vaginal moisturizers and lubricants may help. Choose products that don't contain glycerin because women who are sensitive to this chemical may experience burning and irritation. If a vaginal lubricant isn't enough, many women benefit from the use of local vaginal estrogen treatment, available in cream, vaginal tablet, or ring. Check with your healthcare provider.

Weight gain

Many women gain weight during the menopausal transition and after menopause because metabolism slows. Follow the Low Glycemic Diet recommendations listed in the chapter on "Diet, Exercise, & Supplements—What You Should Know." Perimenopausal women may need to eat less and exercise more just to maintain their current weight.

Brain

As estrogen levels vary throughout the lifespan, the risk of depression in women also varies, and not all treatments are appropriate or effective at all times. For example, in adolescence, onset of depression may be associated with onset of puberty, but treating adolescent girls with antidepressants can cause increased risk of suicide. However, there is a strong belief by some practitioners that adolescent girls should receive rigorous medical treatment if they are depressed to help the brain to re-regulate without becoming adapted to a dysregulated state.

In females of childbearing age, mood disturbances associated with menstrual cycles often signal a risk for later full-blown major depression or bipolar disorder. These women are more sensitive to fluctuating hormone levels. In depressed pregnant and postpartum women, risks of treatment versus risks of non-treatment are intricate and require case-by-case evaluation.

In perimenopausal women, vasomotor symptoms such as hot flashes and night sweats may be harbingers of oncoming depression but also may signal the presence of dysregulated hormones and neurotransmitters. Relieving vasomotor symptoms may be a necessary dimension of treating depression. In menopause, response to selected antidepressants may depend on whether the patient is also taking hormone-replacement therapy. **Any successful treatment for depression must be tailored to a woman's reproductive stage of life.**

Depression is not a normal part of aging. However, more than two million of the thirty-four million Americans age sixty-five and older suffer from some form of depression. Other medical problems and lower functional ability of older adults often obscure the degree of impairment. Typically, symptoms such as insomnia, anorexia, and fatigue are reported rather than a depressed mood. Mild to moderate symptoms of depression are often dismissed as an acceptable response to life stress or a normal part of aging. Get advice from your healthcare provider. Don't ignore your symptoms! Remember—the only time that men and women are "equal" for risk of experiencing depressive episodes is prior to puberty and in older age after women have experienced menopause.

Risk factors include death of a loved one, life transitions (such as retirement), social isolation and loneliness, a history of depression, chronic medical illness, being female, single, divorced or widowed, brain disease, alcohol abuse, use of certain medications, and stressful life events.

Even in healthy older women, brain volume begins to decline as estrogen levels fall in the perimenopausal period. This atrophy occurs particularly in the hippocampus and parietal lobe, areas primarily associated with memory and cognition. A similar loss in brain volume does not begin in men until a decade later (around age sixty), most likely because male sex hormone production declines much more gradually with age. In fact, men over the age of sixty have approximately three times more circulating estradiol than women of a similar age.

Research indicates that mild cognitive impairment and depression seem to go "hand-in-hand" which can raise the risk for persistent cognitive impairment and dementia. Vitamin D deficiency is also a factor. A study in the American Journal of Geriatric Psychiatry found that Vitamin D deficiency is associated with low mood and worse cognitive performance in older adults. See the chapter on "Diet, Exercise, & Supplements—What You Should Know" for a detailed discussion about Vitamin D. Other studies have demonstrated that even after there is clinical recovery from depression in an older adult, cognitive impairment continues. This is evidenced by slower processing of information as well as some dysfunction in higher levels of thinking. Poor circulation may be an underlying problem. Disease in the white matter of the brain seems to directly contribute to depression in older people which worsens over time. The serotonin transporter gene may also be a key risk factor.

Regardless of where you fall on the continuum of life, I hope you have caught the vision of how hormones are the fuel for health. They are the chemical messengers that supervise every function in the body, coordinating complex processes like growth, metabolism, and fertility. Hormones can also influence the immune system and even alter behavior. As our hormone levels go down, debilitating diseases such as arthritis, osteoporosis, mental decline, cancer, heart disease, obesity, loss of sex drive, and incontinence go up. There is a great deal of controversy and differing opinions about the role of hormone replacement therapy; however, it is essential to discuss any concerns with your healthcare provider.

The following excerpt was posted on the internet describing one woman's assessment about how to know if you have estrogen issues.

Ways to Know if You Have Estrogen Issues

by Donna, from Emmitsburg, Maryland

- Everyone around you has an attitude problem.
- You're adding chocolate chips to your cheese omelet.
- The dryer has shrunk every last pair of your jeans.
- Your husband is suddenly agreeing to everything you say.
- You're using your cellular phone to dial up every bumper sticker that says, "How's my driving? Call 1-800-."
- Everyone's head looks like an invitation to batting practice!
- Everyone seems to have just landed here from "outer space."
- You're sure that everyone is scheming to drive you crazy.
- The ibuprofen bottle is empty and you bought it yesterday.

Here's a "real" list describing the symptoms of low estrogen:

- Hot flashes
- Night sweats
- Vaginal dryness
- Mood swings (mostly irritability and depression)
- Mental fuzziness
- Vaginal and/or bladder infections
- Incontinence
- Recurrent urinary tract infections
- Vaginal wall thinning
- Decreased sexual response

- Vision changes
- Trouble expressing thought
- Memory loss
- Low HDL (good cholesterol)
- Decreased menstrual bleeding
- Decreased fullness in breast
- Wrinkling of skin
- Losing track of thoughts

Absolute hormone levels appear to be less important than individual sensitivities to changing levels. The hormonal fluctuations driving the physical changes can put a woman at risk for depression. Some women are at greater risk than others, including midlife women with a history of depression or anxiety, postpartum depression, or premenstrual syndrome. Don't ignore your symptoms!

USE YOUR BRAIN TO OVERCOME INSOMNIA

"Meditate within your heart on your bed, and be still."
"I will both lie down in peace, and sleep; For You alone, O Lord, make me dwell in safety."
- Psalm 4:4 & 4:8

Do you have trouble falling asleep? Or perhaps you fall asleep quickly but wake in the middle of the night or early in the morning, well before the time you need to get up. Well, you're not alone! About thirty percent of Americans complain of sleep disruption according to the National Institutes of Health, and approximately ten percent have symptoms of daytime impairment such as feeling fatigued or having low energy that gets in the way of work productivity or enjoyment of friends, family, or hobbies. We may be eating organic foods, a balanced nutritious diet along with appropriate supplements, and exercising regularly, but if we don't get a good night's rest, it's impossible for us to reach our optimal health.

We all want to be able to fall asleep quickly, get a good solid night's rest, and wake up feeling recharged, renewed and reenergized. **But sleep is also essential to restore our body and mind, support our immune system, deal with daily stresses, promote muscle repair, and give ourselves the mental, emotional, and physical energy, and the focus and alertness we need to get through our day.** A number of negative consequences happen almost immediately when we don't get enough sleep. It's not only hard to wake up in the morning, but our performance on the job or at school generally suffers. In addition, it becomes harder to concentrate and focus or even make the easiest decisions. We may become moody, depressed, or irritated and may struggle to stay awake during the day or during our commute home after work. In fact, after just one night of getting less sleep than needed, we reduce our ability to function by over thirty percent.

It's no wonder that Americans now spend over $750 million a year on over-the-counter sleep aids, and over two billion dollars annually on prescription sleeping pills! This is a twenty-three percent increase since 2006 and a sixty percent increase since 2000. Do you find yourself drinking extra coffee throughout the day or taking afternoon naps to "recharge?" Our ability to cope with the challenges that life brings our way becomes increasingly difficult when we've had less than your optimal amount of sleep.

A new mother is particularly prone to insomnia with many weeks of interrupted sleep both prenatally as well as after the baby is born. Additionally, 75-85% of menopausal women experience hot flashes and sweating that can make it difficult to sleep as well. In fact, according to the National Sleep Foundation, approximately 61% of menopausal women have sleep problems. Older men and women can also have sleep difficulties. As we age, there are changes in what is called "sleep architecture." The number of awakenings during the night increases especially in the early morning. The amount of light sleep is increased and the amount of deep sleep and REM (Rapid Eye Movement) sleep is decreased. REM sleep is the period when most of our dreaming occurs.

People who work alternative shifts often have decreased sleep opportunities which can result in a number of health problems. In 2007, the World Health Organization's International Agency for Research on Cancer listed "shiftwork that involves circadian disruption" as a probable carcinogen. Other symptoms and chronic diseases that can worsen as a result of shift work include cluster headaches, heart disease, obesity, substance abuse, diabetes, poor sexual performance, stress, mental disorders, epilepsy, and digestive diseases. Forty-four percent of night shift workers had a higher prevalence of short sleep duration compared with only about twenty-eight percent of day shift workers. Those who work in transportation and warehousing reported the highest prevalence at 69.7% followed by healthcare workers at 52.3%. Decreased sleep opportunities can have a negative impact on our overall health, and if we work the night shift in transportation or healthcare, we have the greatest risk. Getting enough sleep is essential to maintaining optimal health.

THREE FACTORS THAT DETERMINE WHEN WE FALL ASLEEP

There are three important factors that determine when we fall asleep: circadian rhythm, environmental arousal, and sleep deprivation.

Circadian Rhythm: Circadian rhythm refers to the biological clock in each of us or our sleep-wake cycle. There are two competing forces in our brain composed of hormones and neurochemicals which provide this rhythmic schedule to our waking and sleeping. One is called the circadian arousal system which is trying to keep us awake and the other is called the homeostatic sleep drive which is fiercely trying to put us to sleep. Both curves intersect for about one to two hours in the afternoon somewhere between 2:00 and 3:00 p.m. This period of time has been called the nap zone because it is the time that our brain really wants to take a nap! Equal tension exists between these two drives. During this time memory, attention, and problem-solving suffer leading to more car accidents and difficulty giving or attending a lecture. Most of us probably ignore this afternoon drowsiness and simply reach for another cup of coffee. However, a study by NASA showed that when pilots took a twenty-six minute nap it improved their performance by more than thirty-four percent and a forty-five minute nap made that boost in performance last for six hours.

The brain isn't resting when we're sleeping. During REM sleep, brain wave activity is high and it appears that during these stages of deep sleep we are actually reviewing what we've learned during the day. Research has also shown us that if we don't get enough sleep, our performance dramatically declines. One study took people who normally needed eight hours of sleep and instead gave them only four hours. On a memory test their performance dropped to 9% of the control group who were not sleep deprived. So remember, in order to think well, we need to sleep well.

It might seem self-evident, but it is crucial that we sleep in the dark! Urban areas in particular are sometimes lit up almost as much at night as during the day. Even internal sources of light such as from a clock radio can interfere with our sleep. Try to get the bedroom dark enough so that you can't see your hand when you hold it up in front of your face. Install room darkening shades if needed. The alternating cycle of sleeping and waking is related to daylight and darkness. Scientists have only recently begun to understand this cycle. Melatonin plays a key role because it is a hormone that is part of the sleep-wake cycle. When our eye is exposed to light, a nerve pathway from the retina is stimulated. This nerve pathway goes to the hypothalamus in our brain. A special center called the suprachiasmatic nucleus (SCN) works like a clock once it is exposed to the first light each day. It raises body temperature and stimulates the release of cortisol. It also delays the release of melatonin, which is associated with sleep onset, until darkness arrives. Melatonin is a hormone made by the pineal gland in the brain. When darkness occurs, the pineal gland is turned on by the SCN and begins to actively produce melatonin. The rise in melatonin causes us to feel less alert. Elevated levels remain for about twelve hours. During the day, melatonin is barely detectable. In addition to sunlight, artificial light can also prevent the release of melatonin. Our circadian rhythm is set by the hypothalamus in our brain which also controls other physiological functions such as our temperature. This rhythm is easily disrupted due to jet-lag or shift-work. When I fly between the east and west coast, it generally affects my sleep for several days. One solution that has proven helpful is to use a sublingual spray of melatonin about an hour before my new bedtime in order to reset my sleep-wake cycle.

Environmental Arousal: Environmental arousal refers to the stress and excitement of the day as well as any other drugs or herbal preparations that can increase arousal and therefore delay or interrupt the sleep cycle. Stress releases hormones in the body inhibit sleep so try to avoid stressful phone calls or stressful conversations before bedtime. Think through your day and journal your thoughts before lying down. Using the *My Mindful Journal* is a structured format to help organize your thoughts. Journaling helps us to avoid lying awake at night "solving" all the problems of the day. When that happens our brain is in overdrive. Hormonal shifts during the menopausal time of a woman's life also impact the hypothalamus and temperature regulation which can result in "night sweats" and ultimately impact our sleep as well. Mindfulness breathing can help us bring our attention to the present, both externally and internally, evoking the relaxation response. Learn how to do mindfulness breathing in the chapter "How Brain Strain Sabotages Your Emotional Health—Is Your Brain on Strike?"

Caffeine and alcohol can also interfere with our sleep. According to the American Academy of Sleep Medicine, it takes about thirty to sixty minutes for caffeine to reach its peak level in our blood. One study found increased alertness can begin in as few as ten minutes. However, **it takes about six hours for our body to process only fifty percent of the caffeine in a cup of coffee.** This means that if we drink a cup of coffee at 4:00 p.m. containing 100 mg. of caffeine, by 10:00 p.m. there is still 50 mg of caffeine in our body. The remainder can linger for eight to fourteen hours. And don't forget that caffeine is also found in chocolate and tea. However, not everyone is affected the same way by caffeine. Women generally metabolize caffeine faster than men, but if a woman is taking birth control pills, she metabolizes it at about one-third the rate of women not taking the pill. Smokers tend to process caffeine twice as quickly as non-smokers, and Asians process caffeine the slowest of any race. In terms of alcohol, drinking a glass of wine with dinner is fine provided there are several hours before bedtime. It takes about an hour per drink to process the alcohol. So if you are drinking two glasses of wine, be sure that you're up for at least two hours afterward. In addition, it is important to know that the alcohol-containing "night cap" that is often used for falling asleep will result in a night of shallow, unsatisfying sleep. What happens is that we fall asleep more quickly but the alcohol interferes with our rapid eye movement or REM sleep. A review of twenty-seven studies showed that alcohol does not improve sleep quality. REM sleep is considered to be restorative and it is the time when we dream. A disruption to REM sleep can cause daytime drowsiness and poor concentration. Alcohol can also lead to sleep apnea by suppressing our breathing.

Sleep Deprivation: Finally, studies have shown that when we are deprived of sleep for one day, we go to sleep sooner and stay asleep longer. However, prolonged sleep deprivation can lead to a myriad of problems such as irritability, a lack of motivation and poor performance, a decrease in cognitive ability, and in extreme situations can lead to psychosis including hallucinations, delusions, disorganized thinking, and personality changes. During World War II both the Soviet KGB and the Japanese used sleep deprivation techniques on their prisoners.

EIGHT QUESTIONS ABOUT SLEEPING HABITS

Here are eight questions to ask about sleeping habits:

1. How realistic are my goals for falling asleep and staying asleep?
2. Are there medical, emotional, or behavioral problems that may be causing my problem?
3. Have I informed my healthcare provider about all the medications that I am taking that may possibly have stimulating effects which may be adding to any sleep difficulties?
4. How many hours do I normally sleep at night? How do the number of hours of nighttime sleep affect my day and evening wakefulness?
5. What time do I usually fall asleep and when do I wake up?
6. When am I drinking alcohol and caffeine, how regular are my bedtimes, wake-up times and meal times, and how conducive is my bedroom environment for sleep?
7. Do I feel anxious or tense as bedtime approaches or do I spend excessive wakeful time in bed?
8. Have I tried more than one type of FDA-approved insomnia medication at the appropriate dose?

Armed with the answers to some of these questions, we will be better able to discuss our sleep difficulties with our healthcare provider. Keep a *sleep diary* to help see patterns or trends in your sleep cycle. Some of the items to document are: daytime fatigue, minutes spent napping, medication use, time you first tried to go to sleep, how long it took to fall asleep, how many times you woke up, final waking time, hours slept, sleep quality rating, and how refreshed you felt on awakening.

Be proactive in addressing this important problem of sleep disturbance. New mothers especially need to enlist the help of their spouse or another person to care for the baby at least one to two nights per week, even if they are breastfeeding. Missing a night feeding will not interfere with milk flow. If supplementation with formula is not desired, simply express additional milk during the day for supplemental night feedings.

There are three major areas to consider before beginning any type of insomnia treatment:

- Do you have any significant ongoing depression, mood swings, anxiety, or obsessive-compulsive symptoms that impact your sleep?
- Do you have any medical diagnoses that may affect your sleep such as restless legs syndrome, other increased movements during sleep such as periodic leg movements, and snoring or sleep apnea?
- Are you taking any medications either prescribed or self-administered that may be disrupting your sleep such as alcohol, caffeine, stimulants, corticosteroids (including allergy, cold, cough, and asthmatic medications), or beta blockers (such as propranolol, atenolol, metoprolol, carvedilol) to name a few?

NON-DRUG APPROACHES TO CHRONIC INSOMNIA

The American Academy of Sleep Medicine (AASM) published a comprehensive literature review of psychological and behavioral treatments for insomnia. Based on this peer-reviewed evidence, they made the following recommendations for non-drug approaches to chronic insomnia:

- Stimulus control therapy
- Relaxation training
- Cognitive-behavioral therapy for insomnia (CBTi)

Other non-drug approaches include good sleep hygiene, and resetting your physiological clock in delayed sleep phase disorder.

Stimulus Control Therapy

In this approach the strategy is aimed at helping break the association of bed with wakefulness. It combines de-conditioning with slight sleep deprivation to promote successful sleep onset when going to bed. It is beneficial for both primary insomnia as well as insomnia related to anxious thoughts. The strategy is to go to bed when sleepy and remain in bed for no more than ten minutes (twenty minutes if an older adult) without sleeping. If unable to sleep, get up and do something boring. Return to bed only when sleepy. Continue the process of getting up and returning to bed as frequently as necessary until sleepy. Monitor your sleep behaviors for two weeks using a sleep diary. Research found that 70% of people with conditioned insomnia will improve using stimulus control therapy. However, it is not clear whether the success is related to the de-conditioned response at bedtime or the sleep restriction caused by getting out of bed. Regardless of the time of sleep onset, a regular wake-up time must be maintained and napping must be avoided.

Relaxation Training

Like it or not, stress is a fact of life. It is a natural reaction to changes in your life—both happy and sad. Many things create stress including having a baby, driving in traffic, developing a chronic illness, or financial difficulties. What's important is not what causes the stress, but how you react to it. Dr. Hans Selye, an Austrian endocrinologist and one of the pioneers of biological stress refers to four types of stress:

- *Hyperstress:* too much stress, more than one can handle
- *Distress:* negative, threatening stress
- *Eustress:* good stress which helps us to achieve our goals
- *Hypostress:* too little stress or boredom

The stress response is the same no matter what the threat or "stressor." Whether fulfilling responsibilities at work and home, maintaining relationships with others, balancing finances, or moving to a new area, when we feel threatened our bodies are prepared for "fight or flight." Your adrenal glands produce more stress hormones, your blood pressure increases, your metabolism speeds up, and you begin to breathe faster and shallower. For a more detailed discussion about stress, read the chapter on "How Brain Strain Sabotages Your Emotional Health—Is Your Brain on Strike?" Identify whether or not you have any of the physical, behavioral, emotional, or cognitive warning signs.

We all react to stress differently, but if we don't find ways to de-stress either through some type of relaxation strategy, the continued high level of stimulation can wear our bodies down and ultimately lead to illness! The American Academy of Sleep Medicine (AASM) found relaxation training to be one of the top three evidenced-based, non-drug strategies for treating insomnia. Whether you have problems falling asleep or staying asleep, learning some type of relaxation strategy can help reduce both physical and mental arousal at bedtime making falling asleep easier. Some relaxation techniques include relaxation breathing, progressive muscle relaxation, imagery, and mindfulness. These activities should be practiced at a time other than bedtime in order to master the techniques. Daytime practice allows you to bring the techniques to the bedroom in order to promote muscle relaxation and decrease your arousal. Remember—"Practice makes perfect!" Try to set aside twenty minutes of good, deep relaxation everyday.

Sleep Restriction Therapy

One way to relax and understand the difference between tension and relaxation is to learn progressive relaxation. Check out the chapter on brain strain to find out how to do it. Combine this approach with sleep restriction therapy in order to break the association of the bed with being awake. This approach is similar to *stimulus control therapy*. Limit the time you spend in bed to your total estimated sleep time, while still maintaining the same wake-up schedule. Determine how long you are awake each night and advance your bedtime by that amount. For example, if you are only sleeping or about five hours a night and you need to get up at 6:30 a.m., then go to bed at 1:30 a.m. Continue to set your alarm for 6:30 a.m. When you reach the point where you are asleep 90% of the time spent in bed, you can begin to retire a little earlier. Listen to your body but don't fall into the "nap trap" which can decrease the homeostatic drive that helps you fall asleep. Napping can actually perpetuate insomnia!

Sleep Hygiene

The National Sleep Foundation has defined a number of practices to help promote normal, quality, nighttime sleep and full, daytime alertness. You may have heard this concept referred to as sleep hygiene. Some examples of good sleep hygiene include:

Maintain a regular sleep pattern—between seven to nine hours per night. This may vary depending on whether you are experiencing daytime sleepiness (sleep eight to nine hours) or you're having difficulty sleeping at night (sleep seven hours).

Keep caffeine to a minimum, especially after lunch. Caffeine has a six hour half-life and can affect your sleep even if you don't feel wired. Remember that chocolate and tea have caffeine. Also, be aware that alcohol can disrupt your sleep. While initially it may speed the onset of sleep, it disrupts sleep in the second half as the body begins to metabolize the alcohol, causing arousal.

Eat a small snack in the evening if desired but avoid large, heavy meals which can interfere with sleep, especially if you have reflux disorder. Your last meal should be within two to four hours of sleeping since your metabolism doesn't shut down when you sleep.

Exercise during the day but not within a few hours of bedtime. The more active you are, the better your sleep will be. Computer shut off time should be one to two hours before sleep. Computer screens are designed to look like the sun. So, unless you live in Alaska in the summer you probably don't want to be looking at the sun at 10 o'clock at night. A software program called f.lux fixes this problem. It makes the color of your computer screen adapt to the time of day—warm at night and like sunlight during the day. You can download this program for free for Mac OS X, Windows, Linux, iPhone and iPad. The program makes your computer screen automatically look like the room that you're in.

Develop a relaxing evening routine that includes soothing activities as bedtime approaches—reading, listening to music, journaling, or a warm bath. Avoid super-exciting books that tend to keep you awake. Try to avoid emotionally upsetting conversations and activities before trying to go to sleep. Start a bedtime journaling habit. Go over what you've accomplished that day, what problems you've had, and make your to-do list. This will help to put your mind at ease and stop it from working overtime.

Use your bedroom for sleep and sex only—no television or lying in bed reading your tablet or phone (even if you have f.lux). Harvard University recommends avoiding looking at bright screens for two to three hours before bed and spending as much time in bright light during the day as you can.

Avoid exposure to extreme temperatures, disturbing light and disruptive noises when trying to sleep. However, absolute silence can also be disruptive. Consider obtaining a white noise machine.

The most extensively researched, non-pharmacological therapy for insomnia is Cognitive Behavioral Therapy or CBTi.

Cognitive Behavioral Therapy for Insomnia

Cognitive Behavioral Therapy has been shown to be effective when insomnia is coupled with primary emotional disorders such as depression, anxiety, or alcohol dependence. But it has also shown good results with those who have a medical illness such as cancer, pain issues including fibromyalgia, and even with traumatic brain injury. The important thing is to find a trained mental health provider such as a psychiatric nurse practitioner, psychologist, or clinical social worker to guide you through the process of learning appropriate ways of thinking, behavioral interventions, and self-monitoring with a sleep diary. CBTi, as it is commonly referred to, is provided in five to eight sessions over eight to ten weeks. Here is a brief overview of what to expect.

A thorough assessment will be made to determine any underlying conditions such as depression, anxiety, pain, or whether you may need to have a sleep study. Symptoms such as the urge to move your legs (restless leg syndrome), increased kicking behavior at night (periodic leg movements of sleep), or loud or disruptive snoring (obstructive sleep apnea) will be explored. You may also be asked to try and remember when you were consistently sleeping well in order to determine any factors that might be contributing to your sleep difficulties. A basic overview of normal sleep will be reviewed including a discussion of how it changes over the life cycle. Instruction should also be given on keeping a sleep diary.

After reviewing the sleep diary, problems will be discussed and mutual goals set for such things as minutes to sleep onset, minutes of nighttime wakefulness, number of awakenings, etc. Interventions will include such things as reducing the total time in bed to improve sleep efficiency to greater than 90%.

A discussion of your beliefs about sleep is very important as it helps you to reframe any dysfunctional beliefs. An example might be: "If I don't sleep, I can't ________ (work, socialize, take care of the children, etc.). After reviewing the sleep diary the therapist may reframe your response by observing, "You told me that on _________ you had a terrible night, yet you did _________(that presentation, activity with the family, etc.).

You will also be taught various relaxation techniques such as progressive muscle relaxation, relaxation breathing, and guided imagery and be given time to practice the techniques. The more you practice, the easier it will be to use these strategies to help promote sleep when you're in bed.

OVER-THE-COUNTER SLEEP AIDS

Most over-the-counter sleep aids contain antihistamines. They generally work well but can cause some drowsiness with a hangover effect the next day. You also can develop tolerance fairly quickly to the sedative effects resulting in lack of effectiveness. Two examples of sedating antihistamines are Benadryl and Unisom Sleep Tabs. Tylenol PM and ZzzQuil also contain the antihistamine Diphenhydramine HCl. Side effects can include daytime drowsiness, dry mouth, dizziness, and memory problems. Also, if you're taking other drugs that also contain antihistamines—like cold or allergy medications—you could inadvertently take too much. Antihistamine sleep aids aren't recommended if you have closed-angle glaucoma, asthma, chronic obstructive pulmonary disease (COPD), or severe liver disease or urinary retention.

Melatonin

Melatonin plays a key role in managing insomnia because it is a hormone that is part of the sleep-wake cycle. As we already discussed, a special center called the suprachiasmatic nucleus (SCN) in your hypothalamus works like a clock once it is exposed to the first light each day by raising your body temperature, stimulating the release of cortisol, and delaying the release of melatonin, which is associated with sleep onset. When darkness occurs, the pineal gland is turned on by the SCN and begins to actively produce melatonin. The rise in melatonin causes you to feel less alert. Elevated levels remain for about twelve hours, but during the day, melatonin is barely detectable.

Synthetic melatonin is available over-the-counter, without a prescription. Taking a typical dose of 1.0 mg. to 3.0 mg. may elevate your normal blood levels by one to twenty times. Melatonin supplements are sometimes used to treat jet lag or temporary sleep problems. Scientists are also researching using melatonin supplements to treat Seasonal Affective Disorder (SAD), to help control sleep patterns for night shift workers, to reduce problems with sleeping after surgery, and to reduce chronic cluster headaches. Taking a low-dose melatonin supplement is safe; but, some people may experience side effects such as morning grogginess, vivid dreams, and small changes in blood pressure. However, if you discontinue use, the side effects will stop. A spray dose of melatonin is generally more effective than taking it in tablet form. The melatonin is immediately absorbed sublingually under your tongue and can bypass the normal digestion process. Take the melatonin about one hour before bedtime.

Valerian

Valerian is an herb whose root is used to treat insomnia as well as other conditions such as anxiety, migraines, menstrual cramps, and hot flashes. Some people who have difficulty withdrawing from using prescription sleeping pills use valerian to help them sleep after tapering their sleeping pill dose. It acts like a sedative on the brain and nervous system. Valerian has many interactions with other medications and you should always consult your healthcare provider before using it. It is likely safe for short-term use but should be avoided during pregnancy or while breastfeeding since its safety is not known. Side effects can include headache, excitability, uneasiness, and even insomnia! Scientific studies support taking valerian thirty minutes to two hours before bedtime for twenty-eight days. The dose should be gradually reduced when stopping this herb. Some research suggests that valerian does not relieve insomnia as fast as prescription sleeping pills and can take up to four weeks for any effect to be noticed.

PRESCRIPTION SLEEPING PILLS

Sleeping pills are sometimes helpful when you are traveling or if other disruptions are interrupting your sleep. However, if you have chronic insomnia, it is better to remove the cause and change your lifestyle. An underlying medical condition or sleep disorder should be treated first since insomnia may be just a symptom of another problem. Prescription sleeping pills generally fall into two categories—those that help you fall asleep and those that help you stay asleep. The most common prescription drugs that help you fall asleep include: eszopiclone (Lunesta), ramelteon (Rozerem), triazolam (Halcion), zaleplon (Sonata), and zolpidem (Ambien, Edluar). The most common prescription drugs that help you stay asleep include: estazolam, eszopiclone (Lunesta), temazepam (Restoril), zolpidem (Ambien CR), and doxepin (Silenor). A lower dose form of zolpidem was recently approved by the FDA which is marketed as Intermezzo. It is shorter-acting than Ambien meaning that the effects last for a shorter period of time. This is a sublingual tablet used to treat insomnia characterized by middle of the night awakening with difficulty returning to sleep. You know the symptoms . . . you awaken at 2:00 a.m. and watch the clock creep forward every fifteen or twenty minutes. No matter what you do, you're still lying awake by 4:00 a.m. This medication should only be used if there are at least four hours of bedtime remaining. The recommended maximum dose of Intermezzo is 1.75 milligrams for women and 3.5 mg for men, taken once per night. The recommended dose for women is lower because women clear zolpidem from the body at a lower rate than men. Another new medication just approved by the FDA is called Belsomra. It treats insomnia by temporarily blocking chemicals known as orexins that control the sleep-wake cycle and keep people awake at night. Belsomra alters the signaling action of orexin in the brain. It has been approved for four different strengths: 5, 10, 15, and 20 mg. The lowest effective dose can reduce the risk of side effects including next morning drowsiness. The FDA is requiring that patients who are prescribed Belsomra receive a medication guide detailing the drug's potential safety issues, including sleep-walking, sleep-driving and other semi-awake activities. However, all prescription sleeping pills carry various side effects and considerations which you should thoroughly discuss with your healthcare provider especially if you are pregnant or breast-feeding. Older adults may have an increased risk of nighttime falls and may need a lower dose.

There are certain antidepressants when taken in lower doses may ease insomnia; however, this use is not approved by the FDA. Two common antidepressants that are sometimes prescribed for insomnia are trazodone (Oleptro) and mirtazapine (Remeron). Trazadone may not be a good choice if you have a history of high blood pressure. It also interacts with many other medications. Mirtazapine is sometimes prescribed in older adults to help with weight gain, depression, and insomnia. But it may cause daytime drowsiness as well as interact with many other medications.

It is important to remember to only take sleeping pills when you've completed your evening activities and are ready for bed. Take them about fifteen minutes before you plan on sleeping and get into bed immediately! Avoid drinking alcohol while taking sleeping pills because even a small amount of alcohol increases the sedative effects of the pills and can cause dizziness and confusion. Since you won't know how the sleeping pills will affect you, always start a new prescription on a night that you can sleep in the next day. For example, take it on a Friday night if you're off from work on the weekend. When you're ready to discontinue taking your sleeping pills, it is important to stop your medication gradually. You may find that you have some rebound insomnia for a few days. Be sure to consult with your healthcare provider before weaning off your medication.

Insomnia is a very complex medical problem which is closely tied to our mind. The Apostle Paul spoke about being *"in sleeplessness often"* (II Corinthians 11:27). Getting a good night's rest is a challenge for many people; however, as we discussed there are many strategies that can help. Psalm 4:4 says, "Meditate within your heart on your bed, and be still." Practice relaxation techniques including mindfulness breathing, progressive muscle relaxation, reciting memorized Scriptures, and prayer. My grandfather always said that prayer helped him to get back to sleep when he awoke in the night. After only a short time in prayer, the peace of God would comfort his mind and he would be fast asleep.

The Psalmist also relates the fact that while lying in bed he calls to remembrance songs in the night, (Psalm 77:6). Sounds like a good cure for insomnia! A cell phone or tablet with some ear phones can help. Listen and meditate on some quiet hymns. Reflect upon the words and allow the Holy Spirit to quiet your mind. Or use a Bible app and set it to read a portion of Scripture. One night I meditated on the entire book of Romans!

Practice good sleep hygiene including getting f.lux for your computer and other electronic devices. Turn off computers, tablets, and televisions at least one hour before bedtime and start a relaxing bedtime routine. Start a sleep diary to help you see patterns or trends in your sleep cycle. Write in a journal before going to bed each night to clear your mind of the day's events. For a semi-structured format consider using the *My Mindful Journal*. Ensure that your bedroom is as dark as possible to promote melatonin production. If you are still having problems, seek professional help. **Only six percent of the twenty million Americans suffering from insomnia**

ever consult a healthcare provider to specifically address sleep issues. Don't be one of the statistics! Getting enough sleep is essential to maintaining optimal health.

DIET, EXERCISE, & SUPPLEMENTS—WHAT YOU SHOULD KNOW

"Success doesn't happen overnight. Keep your eye on the prize and don't look back."
–Erin Andrews

Entire books have been written describing healthy diets, exercise programs and important supplements. However, there are a few guiding principles that will help you sort out the important details to support optimal health.

ESSENTIAL FATTY ACIDS

The brain weighs about three pounds and consists of nearly sixty percent fat. The vast majority is a fatty acid called DHA or docosahexaenoic acid. Therefore, in order for our brain cells to perform at peak levels and continue to stay healthy, they need to be nourished regularly with essential fatty acids (EFAs). Fatty acids are critical components of our nerve cell membranes and play an important role in the communication between nerve cells. EFAs are also required to build brain structure, but our bodies can't manufacture them. They must be obtained from dietary sources or supplements. However, **recent statistics indicate that nearly 99% of people in the United States do not eat enough omega-3 fatty acids.**

Essential fatty acids (EFAs) include both omega-3 fats and omega-6 fats. Omega-3 fats are high in EPA (eicosapentaenoic acid) and DHA (docosahexaenoic acid). EPA and DHA have different functions, with EPA mainly affecting mood and behavior and DHA mainly affecting brain development. DHA is like brain nutrition. Results from a recent study suggested that people with higher blood levels of DHA were less likely to show signs of dementia and were more likely to have a larger hippocampus, the region of the brain associated with memory. DHA deficiency has been linked with many psychiatric disorders such as depression, suicidal behavior, anger, and hostility. Deficiencies in DHA have been shown to lower the level of dopamine and the dopamine receptor D2 in the frontal lobe, which can result in problems with attention and learning.

Although some omega-6 fats are good for your health, the balance of omega-6s to omega-3s is essential and should be in a ratio from 1:1 to 4:1. However, the current Western diet is too high in omega-6 fats with a ratio ranging from more than 15:1 to 25:1! Major offenders include processed and fast foods and polyunsaturated vegetable oils - corn, sunflower, safflower, soy, and cottonseed, for example. These oils tend to increase inflammation, an important component of the immune response, heart disease, depression, blood clotting, and cell reproduction. Excessive amounts of omega-6 polyunsaturated fatty acids (PUFA) and a very high omega-6/omega-3 ratio can promote the development of many diseases, including cardiovascular disease, stroke, cancer, and inflammatory and autoimmune diseases such as inflammatory bowel disease, lupus, and rheumatoid arthritis. Depression is also now known to be associated with chronic low-grade inflammation. On the other hand, increased levels of omega-3 PUFA or a lower omega-6/omega-3 ratio have been shown to suppress these conditions.

Some important dietary sources of omega-3 fatty acids are:

- Fatty fish including salmon, fresh tuna, halibut, trout, herring and sardines
- Fortified dairy and juices, such as eggs, milk, and yogurt
- Fresh produce such as brussel sprouts, kale, and spinach
- Grains, nuts, and oils such as flaxseed, walnut, cod liver oil, and soybean oil

Alpha-linolenic acid or ALA is the parent molecule of omega-3 fatty acids. It is derived from plant sources like flaxseed and green leafy vegetables such as spinach. Although it was long believed that the conversion of ALA to the longer chain EPA was very small, recent research in Nutrition Reviews supported the finding that eight to twenty percent of ALA is converted to EPA in humans and between 0.5 and nine percent of ALA is converted to DHA. DHA can also be derived directly from microalgae, making it important for vegans. It is also significant to note that women of reproductive age showed a conversion rate of ALA to EPA 2.5 times greater than the rate in healthy men.

The standard recommendation of consuming two 4-ounce servings of fatty fish per week will provide adequate levels of essential fats. An easier dietary alternative is consuming two tablespoons of ground flaxseed – also known as milled flaxseed or flax meal - per day. Develop a habit of adding two tablespoons of flaxseed to the food that you normally eat such as oatmeal, smoothies, yogurt, or soup. You can also add flaxseed to dark sauces and meat dishes such as chili, stew, or meatballs. Stir in two to four tablespoons per 4-servings. Another way to add ground flaxseed to your diet is to substitute ¼ to ½ cup of the flour in a recipe calling for two or more cups of flour or simply add a couple of tablespoons to pancake batter. Ground flaxseed is kept best in the freezer to prevent it from oxidizing and losing its nutritional potency.

To ensure that you are getting at least the recommended amount of EFAs, it is important to supplement your diet with additional omega-3 fatty acids. You should take a daily supplement containing at least 250-500 mg of omega-3 fatty acids. The strength of the product may read 1000 mg fish oil but may only have 200 mg of omega-3 fatty acids. Healthy adults should also consume 240 to 1000 mg. of DHA everyday to protect their brain health. Pregnant or breastfeeding women should consume a minimum of 300 mg. of DHA daily to promote optimal development of their child's nervous system.

Krill oil is an omega-3 supplement that provides a dose of omega-3s in the form of EPA and DHA, along with phospholipids and astaxanthin, an antioxidant. Phospholipids are important molecules that provide structure and protection to our body's cells. Antioxidants are scavengers that help to prevent cell and tissue damage that could lead to disease. They protect the body against the destructive effects of free radicals that are produced in the body by natural biological processes or introduced from such things as tobacco smoke, toxins, or pollutants. Krill oil claims to be more readily absorbed than regular fish oils due to the oil being delivered in phospholipid form, which are like little packages that transport the fatty acids directly to your cells where they can be immediately used. These phospholipids are the safest and most effective carriers of EPA and DHA and carry no fishy aftertaste or reflux which perhaps you have experienced from regular fish oil! Fish oil is also perishable and can easily go rancid. In fact, it should be refrigerated to help preserve the shelf life. On the other hand, the antioxidants in krill oil ensure that the fish oil does not oxidize easily. This combination of antioxidants with the fish oil is important because oxidation leads to the formation of unhealthy free radicals which can cause cell damage, DNA mutation, and contribute to cardiovascular disease and cancer. Consider adding krill oil as an essential fatty acid supplement.

Besides building your brain structure, essential fatty acids also impact your emotions by playing an important role in both the forming and the functioning of the brain's neurotransmitters, or chemical messengers. In addition, a number of neuropsychiatric disorders may also be influenced by essential fatty acids, including attention deficit hyperactivity disorder (ADHD), Alzheimer's disease, schizophrenia, bipolar disorder, and depression. The American Psychiatric Association (APA) recommends two servings of fatty fish per week, and advises 1000mg (1 gram) of omega-3s (EPA+DHA) per day for patients with mood, impulse-control, or psychotic disorders. The APA also advises that people with mood disorders may benefit from taking one to nine grams per day (1000 to 9000 mg.), adding that doses over three grams per day should be prescribed by a physician.

Omega-3s have also been found to play a role in the protection of the brain against depression as well as provide support for certain premenstrual symptoms. The phospholipids found in krill oil work together with DHA and EPA to reduce the discomfort associated with PMS and exert a balancing effect on certain, important brain neurotransmitters that affect the emotional and psychological aspects of PMS. Research studies have demonstrated that women consuming krill oil experienced less abdominal swelling and discomfort during the menstruation cycle. It has been shown to help alleviate cramps, water-retention and mild mood changes associated with PMS.

LOW-GLYCEMIC DIET

Carbohydrates play an important role in emotional wellness. They provide glucose which is our body's primary energy source. Carbohydrates also promote the production of serotonin. While low-carbohydrate diets can exacerbate depression, diets rich in low-glycemic carbohydrates support positive brain chemistry and moods, according to a research review published in the *Indian Journal of Psychiatry* in 2008.

A low-glycemic diet emphasizes carbohydrate-containing foods and meals that have a mild impact on your blood sugar levels. Glycemic Index or GI Index is a ranking of carbohydrates on a scale from 0 to 100 according to the extent to which they raise blood sugar levels. It measures how much our blood glucose increases after eating.

Low-Glycemic Index foods (with GI Index less than 55) produce a small rise in blood sugar and insulin levels. Some examples include beans, cruciferous vegetables - broccoli, cauliflower, brussel sprouts, - yogurt, grapefruit, apples, and tomatoes.

Intermediate-Glycemic Index foods (with GI Index between 55 and 70) include most types of pasta, bulgur, baked beans, yams, green peas, sweet potatoes, orange juice, and blueberries.

High-Glycemic Index foods (with GI numbers more than 70) make our blood sugar and insulin levels rise quickly. Potatoes, refined white and wheat bread, raisins and other dried fruit, bananas, carrots and watermelon are examples of high-glycemic index foods. There are numerous charts available on the internet as well as phone apps listing foods and their glycemic index. An excellent resource is the University of Sydney's GI website http://www.glycemicindex.com. Remember—low-glycemic index carbs are good for your mental health!

When using the glycemic index as a guide to our food choices, we also have to consider "glycemic load," a measure of how many grams of carbohydrate a normal serving contains. Foods with a low-glycemic load rank from 1-10; those with a medium load range from 11-19, and those with a high-glycemic load rank at 20 or above. **A food may have a high-glycemic index but a low-glycemic load.** For example, although carrots rank high on the glycemic index, (GI = 71), the amount of carbohydrates you would actually consume in a normal serving (½ cup) is pretty low, only 6 grams. Beets are another example. Unless we eat huge portions of carrots or beets, those vegetables will not disturb our blood sugar very much, and they provide important phytonutrients. To calculate glycemic load, simply multiply the number (in grams) of the carbs you would consume in a serving by the food's ranking on the glycemic index. Multiply the GI Index as a percentage rather than a whole number. The glycemic load for carrots ranges from two to four which puts them in the low range.

To drive home the point, here are some examples of refined foods, their glycemic index (GI), and their glycemic load (GL):

- Shredded Wheat Cereal—GI: 69; GL: 57
- Bagel—GI: 72; GL: 38.4
- Cornflakes—GI: 84; GL: 72.7

Now here are some examples of fruits and vegetables:

- Beets, boiled—GI: 64; GL: 6.3
- Bananas—GI: 53; GL: 12.1
- Sweet Potatoes—GI: 54; GL: 13.1

Even though the glycemic index of both food groups are in the medium- to high-glycemic range, the glycemic load of the fruits and vegetables are considerably lower than the glycemic load of the refined grains, even refined whole grains such as shredded wheat. Always consider glycemic index as well as glycemic load when choosing foods. That's the reason why increasing your intake of fruits and vegetables each day and minimizing processed foods is so important.

Research has shown that eating low-GI foods can improve not only our brain health, but our overall physical health, including diabetes and heart health. Low-GI foods help us to manage our glucose and lipid levels as well as reduce insulin levels and insulin resistance. Consuming these types of foods help us to manage our weight because they help control appetite and delay hunger. According to a large prospective study in the *American Journal of Clinical Nutrition*, a diet high in carbohydrates with high-glycemic indexes (GI) were linked to the risk of coronary heart disease development in women. Conversely, low-GI diets are associated with high HDL cholesterol (good cholesterol) concentrations, especially in women.

Evidence also suggests that limiting sugar intake to control blood sugar levels is an important approach to depression. This would include addressing hyperglycemia (high blood sugar), hypoglycemia (low blood sugar), or reactive hypoglycemia (low blood sugar that occurs within four hours of eating). To adopt a low-glycemic dietary lifestyle, replace refined carbohydrates, such as enriched breads, pasta, cereals and snack foods, with whole grains, fruits and vegetables. Rather than three large meals per day, eat small meals four to six times daily. Eat a balance of healthy proteins, fats, and complex carbohydrates at every meal and decrease caffeine intake. To help manage hypoglycemia, supplement with magnesium and chromium and practice relaxation techniques.

TRYPTOPHAN-RICH DIET

Tryptophan is an essential amino acid that promotes serotonin and niacin production in our brain. Maintaining serotonin levels is critical for both mood and sleep. Niacin, or Vitamin B3, is important for overall good health, and in higher amounts has been shown to improve cholesterol levels and lower our risk for heart problems. However, there is a bit of a domino effect. In order for tryptophan to be changed into niacin, the body needs to have enough iron, Riboflavin and Vitamin B6—a strong case for multivitamin and mineral supplementation.

Some people supplement with L-tryptophan to help with sleep, mood disorders such as depression, bipolar or obsessive compulsive disorders, or help to ease the mood swings associated with PMS and PMDD. Although research has shown that people with depression have low levels of L-tryptophan, there is little evidence to show that supplementation really helps and supplements are linked with serious potential side effects. Some of these side effects are blurred vision, dizziness, drowsiness and fatigue, head twitching, hives, nausea, loss of muscle coordination, stiffness, tremors, heart palpitations, and sweating. If you choose to supplement, do not take L-tryptophan if you are taking certain antidepressants such as SSRIs (e.g. sertraline or Zoloft, fluoxetine or Prozac, paroxetine or Paxil, etc.) or MAO inhibitors (e.g. isocarboxazid or Marplan, phenelzine or Nardil, selegiline or Emsam, and tranylcypromine or Parnate). Doing so may lead to a life-threatening condition called serotonin syndrome. Symptoms of serotonin syndrome are increased body temperature, severe muscle spasms, delirium, and coma. New research is beginning to surface, however, regarding the use of L-tryptophan supplements for sleep apnea, Seasonal Affective Disorder, and even smoking cessation.

You can get all the L-tryptophan that your body needs by eating a healthy, balanced diet. Valuable sources of tryptophan include pumpkin, sesame, and sunflower seeds, dairy products, bananas, peanuts, beans, lentils, meat, poultry, seafood, cereal grains, corn and tofu. Turkey is probably the most well-known source of tryptophan. A four ounce portion of either turkey or chicken breast provides 350 to 390 milligrams of tryptophan. Shrimp, tuna, halibut, salmon, cod, and scallops contain between 250 to 400 milligrams of tryptophan.

Since complex carbohydrates help your brain use tryptophan for serotonin production, consume tryptophan-rich foods with whole grains or starchy vegetables. Grilled salmon served on whole grain bread or old-fashioned oatmeal prepared with milk is an example of tryptophan-rich, balanced meal.

MEDITERRANEAN DIET

Evidence also suggests that an anti-inflammatory Mediterranean Diet may help prevent or manage depression. A Mediterranean diet is rich in omega-3 fatty acids and antioxidants which serve as a foundation for both brain health and heart health. Generally, however, we need to add targeted dietary supplements for maximum response. Individuals with depression may consume too many inflammatory omega-6 fatty acids and saturated fats, so increasing consumption of omega-3's and decreasing consumption of trans-fats, saturated fat, and excess omega-6 fatty acids is essential.

The Mediterranean diet emphasizes fresh, colorful fruits and vegetables with most meals, beans and legumes, whole grains, and monounsaturated fats such as olive oil and red wine. This diet is low in processed foods and saturated fat. Are you beginning to see a pattern of the types of foods that are important to include in our diet? The Mediterranean diet also encourages eating with loved ones and enjoying our meals—factors that may enhance our emotional wellness. Fatty fish, such as salmon, albacore tuna, halibut, herring, lake trout and flounder is encouraged in place of high-fat meat. Fatty fish contain omega-3 fatty acids or healthy fats that promote brain function and may reduce symptoms of depression.

EXERCISE

According to the HEALTH factor, an acronym for promoting optimal health, the letter "E" stands for exercise—the energy for wellness. Exercise is good not only for our body but it helps keep our brain sharp. It increases and deepens blood vessels which bring glucose to our brain for energy and oxygen to absorb toxic free radicals. It also promotes neuroplasticity or the growth of new connections between brain cells by stimulating an important protein called brain-derived-neurotrophic-factor (BDNF). BDNF acts as a kind of "Miracle-Gro for the brain," a phrase coined by Harvard psychiatrist, John J. Ratney MD. It links our thoughts and emotions with movement. We know that stress reduces BDNF levels and that people with untreated Major Depressive Disorders have low levels of BDNF. This reduction can be prevented by treatment with antidepressants as well as with aerobic exercise. We also know that exercise increases blood flow to a specific area of the brain's hippocampus which aids in memory formation. Exercise also promotes the release of hormones, all of which provide a nourishing environment for the growth of new brain cells. The Mayo Clinic lists seven benefits of exercise: controlling weight, combating health conditions and diseases, improving mood, boosting energy, promoting better sleep, enhancing sex life, and just generally having fun!

It has been said that "sitting is the new smoking." An increased risk of diabetes, cardiovascular disease, and early death has been linked to the increased time we spend sitting each day. Vladimir Friedman, DC, CCSP, a sports chiropractor, compares sitting to time spent in a cast. When muscle tissue is immobile, it shortens, shrinks, and weakens over time. Standing, squatting, or taking a walk uses your own body weight to help strengthen your muscles. Any movement will bring hydration and nutrients to your tissues to help keep them healthy. To reach our optimal health, we need to engage in four different types of exercise: endurance/aerobic exercise, strength training, balance, and flexibility.

Aerobic exercise increases our breathing and heart rate with the goal of improving the functioning of our cardiovascular and respiratory systems. It also helps our brains in multiple ways by increasing our problem-solving, planning, and attention. In addition, it promotes the growth of cells in our hippocampus, an area of the brain responsible for learning and memory. By improving our overall fitness, research has demonstrated that we can delay or prevent many diseases including heart disease, diabetes, Alzheimers and other dementias. Find an activity that you can enjoy and be sure to follow the American Heart Association's recommendation of doing thirty minutes, five to seven days per week. Some examples of aerobic exercise include: brisk walking or jogging, swimming, dancing, yard work, biking, climbing stairs, or playing a sport such as tennis or basketball. Even cleaning the house can be classified as aerobic exercise! The key is to find something that you enjoy doing and schedule a consistent time on your calendar.

Using a Rate of Perceived Exertion (RPE) chart can help you determine the appropriate level of exercise intensity. An RPE of one is very light—such as walking to your car—while level ten represents maximal exercise. At this level it would be difficult, if not impossible, to talk. If you are too breathless to talk, you should slow down. While doing aerobics aim for about a level five, a level that allows you to talk while doing physical activity but increases your heart rate to your target zone. If you can sing while exercising, you may need to increase the intensity of your exercise to reach the target zone.

The "target" heart rate zone is between 65-85% of your maximum predicted heart rate. In order to calculate Heart Rate Training Zone, you first need to calculate your Maximum Heart Rate. This is determined by your age: 220 – Age = Maximum Heart Rate. For example, a 55-year-old would have the following calculation for Maximum Heart Rate. 220 – 55 years = 165 beats per minute (bpm). This person's target heart rate zone is 107 bpm (65%) to 140 bpm (85%). Exercising at this level will provide a moderate level of intensity that will improve both aerobic capacity and burn fat.

The goal is to progress the intensity of your exercise routine. The three methods for challenging your aerobic fitness are increasing the speed, increasing the resistance, and increasing the duration. According to the Cleveland Clinic, by consistently following an aerobic exercise routine, we will improve our cardiovascular conditioning, decrease our risk of heart disease, lower our blood pressure, increase our HDL or "good" cholesterol, help to better control our blood sugar, manage our weight, improve our lung function, and decrease our resting heart rate. With all these benefits, make it your goal to "get moving" everyday.

Strength training is a second type of exercise. It not only boosts our strength, it tones our muscles, helps prevent osteoporosis, and even helps us lose fat. Just a small increase in strength can make a big difference in our ability to remain independent and carry out our activities. Lifting weights, using resistance bands, or doing push-ups and lunges are some ways to do strength training. A single set of twelve repetitions or less using the appropriate amount of weight can build muscle as efficiently as multiple sets of the same exercise. To give our muscles time to recover, rest a day between exercising each specific muscle group. Many helpful strength training routines are available on the internet and phone apps.

Balance is another form of exercise. Balance exercises can help us prevent falls, especially as we get older. A good way to work on balance is to stand on one foot. I have found that by doing this while brushing my teeth, I consistently practice my balance and I have the sink to grab onto if need be. A piece of equipment known as a BOSU ball is also an excellent way to work on your balance. Other balance exercises include heel-to-toe walking and Tai Chi. Tai Chi originated in China as a martial art. There are more than 500 studies about the various physical benefits of Tai Chi from improving balance and attention span, to boosting the immune system, helping with arthritis symptoms, and insomnia. It is slow motion and low impact, but it carries a big punch. The movements are usually circular and never forced, the muscles are relaxed rather than tensed, the joints are not fully extended or bent, and connective tissues are not stretched. Research studies have found that Tai Chi has increased mineral bone density, boosted endurance, strengthened the lower body, and even eased depression. It teaches people to move well in multiple planes of motion with a state of awareness. Taking a class may be the best way to learn Tai Chi. Why not try out a class in your local area and see if your balance doesn't improve?

Flexibility is the fourth type of exercise. It involves stretching our muscles to help our bodies remain limber. It enhances the range of motion of our joints and helps nutrients reach our muscles after exercising. Long hours at a computer and poor posture can shorten our muscles over time. Flexibility training gives us more freedom of movement for other exercises and for our everyday activities. Yoga as well as simply stretching key muscle groups can help improve our flexibility. Hold stretches for ten to thirty seconds and yoga poses for up to five minutes.

Spiritual Exercise

There is one more type of exercise that is critical to attaining optimal health and that exercise is spiritual exercise. Spirituality helps us reframe our situation based on our beliefs. It gives meaning and purpose to our existence. Keeping a journal is a great way to crystalize our thoughts and promote spiritual growth. Learn to focus on appreciation and thankfulness even during times of frustration and stress. Track your progress and journal your accomplishments. You can do this with pen and paper or by using one of the many Smartphone apps available. An additional resource is the *My Mindful Journal* which provides a structured framework to help you reflect on your spiritual progress.

The Bible instructs us in I Timothy 4:7-8, *"Exercise yourself toward godliness. For bodily exercise profits a little, but godliness is profitable for all things."* There are no group classes for spiritual exercise! This is an individual exercise. Many people *"have a form of godliness, but deny the power thereof. . ."* (II Timothy 3:5). These folks are godly "look-alikes." They have an appearance of godliness. They attend religious services and may even talk about God. But they don't really know Him. Focus instead on exercising YOURSELF toward godliness. Break out into a spiritual "sweat." Spiritual exercise takes discipline and requires us to prioritize our time. Faith is like a muscle—the more it is used, the stronger it gets. Our spiritual growth relates directly to our daily discipline of time spent focusing on spiritual principles, including prayer, meditation, fasting, reading and memorizing Scripture, and serving others.

We see an intense example of spiritual exercise by the Lord Jesus as He prayed in the garden of Gethsemane on the night before He was to be crucified. Dr. Luke's gospel tells us that His sweat was like drops of blood: *"And being in agony, He prayed more earnestly. Then His sweat became like great drops of blood falling down to the ground"* (Luke 22:44). This phenomenon is called "hematidrosis." It is a rare, but very real, medical condition where one's sweat will contain blood. The sweat glands are surrounded by tiny blood vessels. These vessels can constrict and then dilate to the point of rupture where the blood will then effuse into the sweat glands. The cause is extreme anguish. In the other Gospel accounts, we see Lord Jesus' level of anguish: *"My soul is overwhelmed with sorrow to the point of death"* (Matthew 26:38; Mark 14:34). Our Savior knew the intensity of individual spiritual exercise.

Hebrews 12:1-2 gives us this instruction, *"Therefore we also, since we are surrounded by so great a cloud of witnesses, let us lay aside every weight, and the sin which so easily ensnares us, and let us run with endurance the race that is set before us, looking unto Jesus, the author and finisher of our faith, who for the joy that was set before Him endured the cross, despising the shame, and has sat down at the right hand of the throne of God."*

What is weighing you down? Is it time constraints or the "tyranny of the urgent" with upside down priorities? How much time do you devote to spiritual exercise each day versus the time spent on other activities? Perhaps your "weight" is addiction—to alcohol, prescription pills, or even food. According to the National Institute on Alcohol Abuse and Alcoholism, thirty percent of Americans engage in risky or unhealthy drinking patterns. If you're a man that means fifteen standard drinks per week, which equates to two drinks per day plus one more each week. For women more than eight standard drinks per week or only one drink per day plus one more each week is considered an unhealthy drinking pattern. A standard drink in the United States is defined as a drink containing about 14 grams of pure alcohol. That equals 12 ounces of beer, 5 ounces of table wine, or 1.5

ounces of 80-proof whiskey. Does your drinking fall into an unhealthy and risky pattern?

Other "weights" which may hinder your spiritual growth might be apathy, jealousy, anger, or anxiety. Are we apathetic or indifferent to the needs of those around us who are outside of our immediate family—our friends, neighbors, or people in the community? Whatever weight is hindering you from maintaining endurance in your spiritual race needs to be "laid aside."

When we seriously train, we willingly undergo hours of discipline and even pain to win the prize. If you believe that this life is not the end of the story, then we have a purpose beyond the time spent in the here and now. Our training for godliness is not in vain. The reason for our "spiritual work-out" is to win the crown! *"Athletes work hard to win a trophy that cannot last, but we do it for a crown that will last forever"* (I Corinthians 9:25, CEV). Both physical exercise and spiritual exercise are essential in reaching and maintaining optimal health.

MEDICAL GRADE MULTIPLE VITAMIN AND MINERAL

Optimal health requires the daily intake of a high-grade vitamin and mineral formulation with significant antioxidant support. For example, iodine is amply available in iodized table salt. However, many people are both cutting down on sodium intake as well as using other types of table salt that do not contain iodine. Iodine is essential for thyroid function and normal brain development. According to a recent study in the *Lancet,* children born to women with even mild to moderate iodine deficiency are at increased risk for lower IQ and reading ability. Unfortunately, not all prenatal vitamins contain an adequate amount of iodine. Women should take a supplement that contains at least 150 micrograms of iodine *and* use iodized salt.

B-complex vitamins are particularly important to your brain health. They serve as cofactors to help the body make neurotransmitters, the chemical messengers of the brain. Inadequate levels of B-vitamins, especially folate, vitamin B12, niacin, and vitamin B6, can disrupt the body's ability to synthesize or manufacture neurotransmitters such as serotonin, dopamine, or norepinephrine. The result can lead to mood alterations and impact our overall brain function, memory, and cognition or comprehension. A report published online on June 2, 2010, in the *American Journal of Clinical Nutrition* reveals a lower risk of developing depression among men and women who consume greater amounts of vitamin B6 and vitamin B12. Additionally, another study with over 3500 participants, as part of the Chicago Health and Aging Project conducted by Rush University Medical Center, revealed that there was no significant benefit observed in obtaining B vitamins from food alone. The study noted that vitamin B12 from food sources has poor bioavailability and absorption. So supplementation is essential!

In 2005, a team of researchers from Yale University examined all the published studies on vitamin B6 and depression. Although not every study showed evidence of benefits from B6 treatment, the researchers did find that premenopausal women suffering from depression benefited from vitamin B6. Another study from Yale University revealed that premenstrual women suffering from depression benefited from taking vitamin B6. And finally, clinical trials have demonstrated that folic acid can relieve depression on its own and enhance the antidepressant effect of conventional antidepressants. In one study, patients given 500 mcg folic acid daily in conjunction with fluoxetine (Prozac) experienced a significant improvement in depressive symptoms compared with patients receiving the antidepressant alone, and women benefited particularly. Because relapse is associated with low serum folate, it is important to maintain folate supplementation for a year following a depressive episode. L-methylfolate (in the 7.5 mg or 15 mg strength marketed as Deplin tablets) is approved by the FDA for the distinct nutritional requirements of individuals who have suboptimal L-methylfolate levels and have major depressive disorder (MDD). It is particularly effective as adjunctive support for individuals who are on an antidepressant.

Vitamin B12

Vitamin B12 deficiency is also very prevalent, particularly in the over-sixty population. When our blood levels of this key nutrient are low, we may experience low energy, mental fatigue, mood changes, and sleep difficulties. In the previous chapter, we discussed the importance of melatonin in treating insomnia. Melatonin has been called the sleep hormone, and B12 plays a key role in the production of melatonin. Vitamin B12 is also essential in converting carbohydrates to glucose—our body's fuel. In addition, it enables our body to convert fatty acids into energy. However, **most multivitamins are a complete waste of money when it comes to their Vitamin B12 quality.** Most of them contain 100 to 200 micrograms of B12 but only one third of one percent is actually absorbed! Only a small fraction of this important vitamin gets absorbed through your gut when you take a pill, tablet, capsule, or gelcap. A better alternative is to take Vitamin B12 separately as a pre-metered non-aerosol spray which is rapidly absorbed from your mouth.

Vitamin D

Vitamin D, or calcitriol, is actually a steroid hormone and not a vitamin. A vitamin is a substance essential to human health that cannot be produced by the body. Vitamin D is certainly essential to the metabolism of calcium and phosphorous and promotes bone mineralization and growth, but it does not meet the second part of the definition since it is produced by our bodies when we're exposed to sunlight. When it is not possible to get adequate exposure to sunlight due to climate or skin cancer risk, supplementation is essential.

There are two widely recognized forms of vitamin D: D3 and D2. Vitamin D3 is generated in the skin when exposed to light energy and D2 is found in various plant sources. However, neither form of vitamin D is usable until it is transformed chemically by either the liver or the kidneys. It eventually becomes 1,25 Dihydroxy vitamin D, a powerful steroid hormone. It is fat soluble and can pass through cell membranes and bind to vitamin D receptors where it has many repair and maintenance functions.

According to Dr. John Cannell, director of the Vitamin D Council, vitamin D affects more than 200 genes in the body and can be found in most body tissues. **Low vitamin D levels have been found to be related to osteoporosis, depression, heart disease and stroke, cancer, diabetes, parathyroid problems, immune function, and even weight loss.** Risk factors for deficiency include:

Age (greater than 65 years old)
Insufficient sunlight
Breastfeeding
Dark skin
Malabsorption diseases
Obesity (BMI greater than 30)
Medications that alter vitamin D metabolism such as anticonvulsants (e.g. anti-seizure, mood stabilizers, and medication for neuropathic pain such as dilantin, depakene, tegretol, Lyrica), and glucocorticoids (e.g. anti-inflammatory medications such as prednisone, dexamethasone, and hydrocortisone)
Liver disease
Kidney disease

In theory, unprotected sunlight exposure should provide sufficient vitamin D. However sunscreens with SPF ratings greater than eight effectively block synthesis of vitamin D in the skin. Older adults are particularly at risk since they often stay inside and have poor diets as well. The 25(OH)D test is the only test that will tell you whether you're getting enough vitamin D.

Optimal serum concentrations of 25(OH)D for bone and general health have not been established; they are likely to vary at each stage of life. However, according to the National Institutes of Health, the following chart shows the acceptable ranges for vitamin D levels:

Serum 25-Hydroxyvitamin D [25(OH)D] Concentrations and Health

nmol/L**	ng/mL*	Health status
<30	<12	Associated with **vitamin D deficiency**, leading to rickets in infants and children and osteomalacia in adults
30–50	12–20	Generally considered **inadequate for bone and overall health** in healthy individuals
≥50	≥20	Generally considered **adequate for bone and overall health** in healthy individuals
>125	>50	Emerging evidence links **potential adverse effects** to such high levels, particularly >150 nmol/L (>60 ng/mL)

* Serum concentrations of 25(OH)D are reported in both nanomoles per liter (nmol/L) and nanograms per milliliter (ng/mL).
** 1 nmol/L = 0.4 ng/mL. **Be sure to check what measurement your lab is using.**

These levels are simply markers of exposure to vitamin D from sun, dietary sources and supplements. Be sure to check your vitamin D level every year. NIH states that research has demonstrated that Vitamin D intakes of 5,000 IU/day achieved serum 25(OH)D concentrations between 100–150 nmol/L (40–60 ng/mL), but no greater. When you supplement, it is recommended that you never exceed that level unless carefully monitored by your healthcare provider.

PROBIOTICS VS. PREBIOTICS

We may not always think about it, but our colon is a very important health organ in our body, containing more than a thousand different bacterial species. In fact, the total numbers of bacteria reach the tens of billions—more than ten times all the cells in our body! The colon is where both probiotics and prebiotics end up. Both prebiotics and probiotics are essential to reach our optimal health. They both help to increase healthy bacteria in our gut, but they do it in different ways. It is only in the last fifteen years that researchers have discovered the role of colon health to our overall wellness.

The idea that there could be an interaction between the brain and gut once seemed totally absurd. Yet now we have increasing scientific evidence that this, indeed, occurs. The bacteria in the lower gut make literally hundreds of chemicals as part of their normal metabolism. Some of these by-products slip through the bowel wall, enter the blood, and travel to the brain. While evidence is still limited in psychiatric illnesses, there are clusters of evidence which point to the possibility that variations in the composition of gut microbes may be associated with changes in the normal functioning of the nervous system. These changes result in not only better psychological health but less age-related decline. A recent study published in *Gut Microbes* discussed the gut-brain axis as it relates to Irritable Bowel Syndrome (IBS). The study identified that patients with Irritable Bowel Syndrome, a prototype of functional gastrointestinal disorders (FGIDs), display altered composition of the bacteria in their gut compared with healthy controls. The study also demonstrated the benefit of using probiotics and antibiotics from both the gastrointestinal as well as the psychological perspective.

Another study from Oxford University fed rats two different types of prebiotics. Both rat groups gained bifodobacteria, beneficial gut bacteria, and showed a significant increase in BDNF, an important protein that helps develop and maintain brain cells. In addition, a brain receptor that plays an essential role in memory, learning and development also grew stronger with prebiotics. Researchers are continuing to gain valuable insights into the complex interactions between the gut and the brain.

Probiotics are vital for establishing and maintaining a healthy population of beneficial intestinal microorganisms, which play an important role in conditions such as obesity, diabetes and metabolic syndrome. Healthy gut flora helps decrease systemic inflammation, support a healthy immune system, balance neurotransmitters, and promote healthy detoxification of hormone metabolites (the end products of hormones that have been broken down by the liver). In recent years, there has been a great deal of television advertising about the benefits of probiotics. Yogurt and other dairy products are a good dietary source of probiotics *if* they contain live active cultures. Fermented products such as sauerkraut are also good dietary sources. Also, consider adding raw, organic, unfiltered apple cider vinegar such as Braggs or Trader Joes to your recipes.

Unfiltered apple cider vinegar is full of probiotics as well as other good bacteria. Some research suggests that if we drink apple cider vinegar with a starchy meal, then the starches we don't digest will feed the good bacteria in our gut. It has an anti-glycemic effect and can block some of the digestion of carbohydrates. The research is “sketchy” on most of the purported benefits of apple cider vinegar. However, one study published recently showed that apple cider vinegar can help control our lipid profile, red blood cell count, and the effects of oxidative stress on our liver and kidney membranes—at least in mice! Use it to make your salad dressing—1 tablespoon vinegar to 2 tablespoons olive oil and seasonings of your choice, or dilute one to two tablespoons in a glass of water and drink it with your meal. If you choose to take a probiotic supplement, your supplement should contain a combination of lactobacillus that mainly resides in the small intestines and bifidobacterium which is most predominant in the large intestines. These bacterium help to normalize overall bowel function and ferment fiber. Probiotic bacteria must be kept alive. It can be killed by heat, stomach acid, or simply die over time. Be sure to keep your supplement refrigerated. Certain probiotic species have been shown to be helpful for childhood diarrhea, irritable bowel disease and for recurrence of certain bowel infections such as C. difficile.

Prebiotics, on the other hand, are a specialized plant fiber that beneficially nourishes the good bacteria already in the large bowel or colon. **This fiber acts like a fertilizer to promote the growth of many of the good bacteria in your gut and provide many digestive and general health benefits.** The healthy bacteria that live there strengthen the bowel wall, improve mineral absorption, and aid in the regulation of hormone production. Prebiotic fiber is found in many fruits and vegetables such as apple skins, asparagus, wild yams, bananas, chicory root, beans, onion, and garlic. The problem is that a serving of each contains only about one to two grams of fiber, falling far short of the recommended 25 grams per day.

Research studies have shown that there are many health benefits to taking a prebiotic supplement: better regularity, improved immune function, increased energy, less leaky gut, more calcium absorption resulting in improved bone density, decreased inflammation, and weight management control. Look for a dietary supplement that contains oligofructose and inulin. These natural plant-based fibers have been shown to nourish the beneficial bacteria in your gut. The mixture of these two fibers is called oligofructose enriched inulin and there has been a great deal of sound scientific research supporting the use of this combination.

The mixture of these two fibers has been found to be more effective in producing beneficial results than either one by itself because it acts on all areas of the colon, not just one localized site. Oligofructose works primarily on the right side of our colon and inulin acts on the transverse and left side, providing overall fertilization of beneficial bacteria. The advantage of taking a prebiotic supplement over a probiotic supplement is that it won't go bad. No refrigeration is needed and it will survive the trip from our mouth to our lower gut intact. We owe it to our overall health and wellness to support our colon and brain health with either probiotics or prebiotics.

BONE LOSS PREVENTION SUPPLEMENTS

We all lose bone mass as we age; however, osteoporosis occurs when bone loss goes beyond what is considered normal. The body attempts to compensate for factors interfering with its normal biochemical balance and bone becomes excessively fragile due to the loss of minerals and its protein matrix. Some of the factors that contribute to this imbalance include poor nutrition, lack of sunlight exposure and low vitamin D levels, high caffeine intake, lack of exercise, inflammation, an acid-forming diet, the use of various prescription medications, and chronic stress. Lack of adequate nutrients either as a result of poor nutrition or a physical condition that prevents the body from absorbing nutrients such as celiac disease and other digestive disorders can contribute to developing osteoporosis. Hormonal imbalances from diabetes, thyroid disorders, menstrual irregularities, or ovary and uterus removal can also lead to poor bone health.

It is important to note that taking high doses of calcium without additional key bone nutrients such as vitamin K can actually increase problems with arterial calcification or "hardening of the arteries." A specific form of vitamin K called K2 or menaquinone (MK-7) is very important in keeping calcium in your bones and out of your arteries! This important information was identified in a large study of 4,800 people called the Rotterdam Study, which showed that those who consumed the most vitamin K2 had a 50% reduced risk of calcification in their arteries. They also had a reduced risk for cardiovascular events during this 10-year period. But beside vitamin K2, we also need vitamin K1. The Framingham Heart Study demonstrated that those with the highest vitamin K1 intake (250 mcg/day, compared to the recommended daily intake of 90 mcg/day) had a threefold reduction in hip fracture risk. You can read more about this study on the National Institutes of Health government website. Be sure to check with your healthcare provider before starting vitamin K, especially if you are taking any type of blood thinner medication such as Coumadin (warfarin), Plavix (clopidogrel), or even aspirin.

There are at least twenty bone-building nutrients essential for optimal bone health which our bodies cannot manufacture. You need balanced amounts of each one to keep your bones strong and healthy. Generally speaking, diet alone does not provide sufficient quantities of these nutrients. When choosing your supplements, choose a medical-grade multivitamin/mineral formulated specifically for bone health. The following list will give you some guidance when choosing a multi-vitamin that will help support your bone health. It is beyond the scope of this book to give a detailed explanation about each of these nutrients; however, I urge you to research the importance of each of them in more depth.

NUTRIENT	DAILY DOSE	DISCUSSION
Calcium	800-1200 mg.	Provides healthy bone development and maintenance. Gives bones both strength and rigidity.
Magnesium	400-800 mg.	Gives strength and firmness to bones and makes teeth harder. Ratio Ca/Mg = 2:1
Chromium	200-1000 mg.	Promotes production of collagen and moderates bone breakdown
Silica	5-20 mg.	Maintain strong, flexible bones.
Phosphorous	800-1200 mg.	Combines with calcium to form a mineral crystal that gives strength and structure to our bones and teeth. Ratio Ca/P = 1:1
Zinc	12-30 mg.	Needed to produce the matrix of collagen protein threads.
Manganese	2-10 mg.	Co-factor in the formation of bone cartilage, bone collagen, and bone mineralization.
Copper	1-3 mg.	Contains enzyme called lysyl oxidase, which aids in the formation of collagen for bone and connective tissue.
Boron	3-5 mg.	Needed for proper metabolism and utilization of calcium, magnesium, vitamin D, estrogen, and perhaps testosterone.
Potassium	4000-6000 mg.	Neutralizes bone-depleting acids; Prevents too much calcium from being excreted in the urine.
Strontium	3-30 mg.	Promotes mineralization of the bones and teeth.
Vitamin D	800-2000 IU	Mobilizes calcium and phosphorus for release from bone in the presence of parathyroid hormone; Promotes intestinal absorption of calcium and phosphate; Increases kidney absorption of calcium and phosphorus.
Vitamin C	500-3000 mg.	Assists in the formation of collagen; Stimulates the cells that build bone; Optimizes functioning of adrenal steroid hormones, which play a vital role in bone health.

NUTRIENT	DAILY DOSE	DISCUSSION
Vitamin A	5000 IU or less	Essential role in the development of osteoblasts, the bone-building cells; Limits calcium absorption and metabolism.
Vitamin B6	25-50 mg.	Necessary for hydrochloric acid (HCl) production by the stomach, which is necessary for calcium absorption. Also important for adrenal function; co-factor in the enzymatic cross-linking of collagen strands; and helps prevent build-up of homocysteine in the body.
Folic Acid	400-1000 mcg.	Detoxification of homocysteine, an amino acid linked with inflammation and increased fracture risk.
Vitamin B12	150-1000 mcg.	Osteoblasts, the body's bone-building cells, require an adequate supply of B12, to function properly.
Vitamin K1	250-1000 mcg.	Required for the synthesis of osteocalcin, the bone protein matrix upon which calcium crystallizes. Serves as the "glue" that binds calcium onto the skeleton.
Vitamin K2	45-180 mcg.	More bioavailable, longer lasting, and provides for greater increase in bone strength. Superior ability of MK-7 over K1 to enhance both bone and heart health.
Fats	20-30% of total calories	Required for proper calcium metabolism; Essential component of all membranes, including cartilage and bone.
Protein	1.0-1.5 g/kg.	Beneficial for intestinal absorption of calcium; A major building block for bone. Too much is detrimental. Leads to a state known as chronic low-grade metabolic acidosis (CLGMA), which actually washes calcium out of the body.

HOPE & HAPPINESS: THE SPIRITUAL FOUNDATION FOR HEALTH

"Now may the God of hope fill you with all joy and peace in believing, that you may abound in hope by the power of the Holy Spirit." -Romans 15:13

Hope and happiness help us to see the big picture and bring meaning to our often chaotic lives. Together they represent the spiritual foundation for health and wellness. "Happy is he who has the God of Jacob for his help, Whose hope is in the Lord his God," (Psalm 146:5). Simply pursuing happiness as an end in itself leads to a *taking attitude*, or giving the self what it wants. Hope on the other hand allows us to put aside our selfish interests and find meaning in Someone or something other than ourselves. The result is a *giving attitude.* Researchers at Stanford University showed that people who have high meaning in their lives are more likely to help others in need.

The physical structure of our brains can actually change over time based on our thoughts, values, attitudes, and beliefs. The scientific body of evidence supporting the impact of spirituality on physical health, emotional well-being, and overall quality of life continues to grow as researchers discover that our brain structure and our thinking are interrelated. **A comprehensive review of the literature that compared spirituality to other health interventions found that people with a strong spiritual life had an 18% reduction in mortality.** Lucchetti, the lead author of one study, concluded that the life-lengthening benefits of spirituality can be compared to eating a high amount of fruits and vegetables or taking blood pressure medication. While some researchers have suggested that the extent of his conclusions about the benefit of spirituality on health is exaggerated, most researchers agree that there is a positive relationship between religious and spiritual practices and better health outcomes.

Our thinking, including our values, attitudes, and beliefs actually change the structure of our brain in multiple ways. This process also works the other way around. Psychologist Donald Hebb coined the phrase, *"Neurons that fire together, wire together."* The connections between neurons are strengthened and the layers in the brain become thicker. Studies about spirituality are notoriously difficult to conduct and have faced criticism over the complexity of trying to scientifically measure subjective attitudes, beliefs, emotions, spiritual practices, coping strategies, and spirituality-based interventions. Although many questions remain unanswered, the evidence continues to grow supporting the impact of spirituality on health and wellness.

Broadly defined, spirituality encompasses all attempts to find meaning, purpose, and hope in relation to the sacred or significant. Spiritual practices include the values, beliefs, practices, or philosophies which impact our thoughts, emotions, and behavior. In this sense, spirituality influences our ability to cope with stress, loss, and illness. It helps us to reframe our situation based on our beliefs. The way that we find meaning in our interactions with other significant people in our lives is also impacted by our spirituality. The Bible tells us in II Timothy 1:7, *"For God has not given us a spirit of fear, but of power and of love and of a sound mind."* As a follower of the Lord Jesus Christ, our values and beliefs shape our lives and give us hope and happiness.

Viktor Frankl, MD, PhD, an Austrian psychiatrist and neurologist, as well as a Holocaust survivor, presents his existential personality theory in his book *The Will to Meaning*. He believed that a healthy individual is primarily motivated by the desire to find meaning and purpose in his or her personal existence. To demonstrate how essential that meaning is to human existence, he reported on his experiences in several Nazi concentration camps during World War II.While working as a therapist in the camps, he encountered two suicidal prisoners. Both were hopeless and thought there was nothing to live for. Frankl helped both men to realize that life was still expecting something from them. For the one, it was his young child who was separated from him and living in a foreign country. For the other man, who was a scientist, it was a series of books that he needed to finish writing. He believed that if a person knows the "*why* for his existence, (he) will be able to bear almost any *how*." He concluded that "the last of the human freedoms (is) to choose one's attitude in any given set of circumstances, to choose one's own way." Whether or not you concur with Dr. Frankl, his viewpoint will give you something to ponder in relation to your own worldview. Corrie ten Boom was another Holocaust survivor and a devout evangelical Christian who helped save hundreds of Jewish lives. She spent her life telling others how hope and happiness as found in the Lord Jesus Christ sustained her through the dark days of concentration camp imprisonment in Ravensbrück, near Berlin, Germany. The Apostle Paul also had a "prison perspective" when he wrote from a Roman prison in Philippians 4:4 "Rejoice in the Lord always; again I will say, rejoice!" Note that our delight is *in the Lord*, not in fluctuating circumstances. He is the One Who gives us meaning and purpose. We know that fear and despair from the circumstances of life can virtually put blinders on our eyes and prevent us from experiencing hope and happiness. Finding meaning in life is an issue that confronts all of us regardless of our age or circumstances.

HOPE

From a Biblical worldview, Romans 15:13 says, "Now may the God of hope fill you with all joy and peace in believing, that you may abound in hope by the power of the Holy Spirit." Hope has its source in "the God of hope." The Bible gives us the solution to the hopelessness that cripples many who suffer from depression. It is found in both the Torah (Deuteronomy 6:5) as well as in the New Testament (Matthew 22:36-38, Mark 12:29-31, Luke 10-26-28) and involves three aspects: intimacy with God, intimacy with others, and self-worth.

Jesus summarized it this way: *"You shall love the Lord your God with all your heart, and with all your soul, and with all your mind, and with all your strength. This is the first commandment. The second is this: you shall love your neighbor as yourself"* (Mark 12:29-31).

INTIMACY WITH GOD

Deep within every human being is a God-vacuum or an inner emptiness that can only be filled by a personal relationship with the Lord Jesus Christ or *Yeshua Ha Mashiach* - the Anointed One. It begins with God reaching out to us. . . not the other way around.

God loves you and wants to have a relationship with you. *"For I know the thoughts that I think toward you, says the Lord, thoughts of peace and not of evil, to give you a future and a hope"* (Jeremiah 29:11, NIV).

Sin has separated us from God. *"All we like sheep have gone astray; we have turned, every one, to his own way; and the Lord has laid on Him the iniquity of us all"* (Isaiah 53:6) and *"There is none righteous, no, not one"* (Romans 3:10). Did you notice that the middle letter of SIN is "I"?

God provided the way to re-establish intimacy with Himself. *"While we were yet in weakness (powerless to help ourselves), at the fitting time Christ died for (in behalf of) the ungodly"* (Romans 5:6, AMP).

We need to repent from our sins and accept His free gift of salvation. Only then can we experience true intimacy with God and experience His hope. *"But now in Christ Jesus you who once were far off have been brought near by the blood of Christ"* (Ephesians 2:13).

INTIMACY WITH OTHERS

Loneliness, or lack of intimacy with others, is a second major source of emotional pain resulting in hopelessness. Women, in particular, are hard-wired by God for relationships with others. Our brain circuits are fueled by estrogen and oxytocin to respond to stress by creating protective social networks and nurturing behaviors. According to the research of Dr. Shelly Taylor and others in 2000, it was observed that women do not only respond to stress by what has been called the *"fight or flight"* reaction. Rather, women respond by seeking connections with others and nurturing behaviors, a phrase coined by Taylor as *"tend and befriend."*

King Solomon acknowledged the importance of intimacy with others by writing the following words in the book of Proverbs. *"Oil and perfume rejoice the heart; so does the sweetness of a friend's counsel that comes from the heart"* (Proverbs 27:9) and *"Just as iron sharpens iron, a person sharpens the character (mind) of his friend"* (Proverbs 27:17).

There are three strategies to build intimacy with others. They include:

Get rid of grudges daily.

Spend time every day getting more intimate with your spouse, children, other close family members. Seek to quickly resolve family conflicts.

Develop one or two close friends to enjoy social activities and share intimate concerns together.

TRUE SELF-WORTH

Self-worth is a measure of our self-image and character. It helps us to believe that we are capable of doing our best with the talents that God has given us. Philippians 4:13 says, *"I can do all things through Christ Who strengthens me."* True self-worth relates to who we are in Christ. It is not exaggerating our qualities which can lead to arrogance or narcissism. Nor is it belittling ourselves and making light of our talents and spiritual gifts which is false pride. Can you relate to these extremes? The Bible gives us this guidance: *"Having predestined us to adoption as sons (and daughters) by Jesus Christ to Himself, according to the good pleasure of His will, to the praise of the glory of His grace, by which He made us accepted in the Beloved (Jesus Christ)"* (Ephesians 1:5-6). Whatever baggage we're carrying, God has accepted us unconditionally and wants to *"conform you to the image of His Son (the Lord Jesus Christ)"* (Romans 8:29). Ask Him. . . and He will do just that!

HAPPINESS

Happiness is the second component in the spiritual foundation for health. According to Princeton University, happiness involves emotions ranging from contentment to intense joy. The Bible adds that *"godliness with contentment is great gain"* (I Timothy 6:6). Everyone seems to be striving for happiness. Whether it is a larger home, a new car, or a better job, we expect that happiness will be the end result. In fact, Aristotle called happiness *"the chief good, the end towards which all other things aim."*

Happiness is one of the "big six" emotions mentioned in the chapter on "The Brain—The Control Center for Emotions." Happiness may be viewed two ways—either as the goal to be pursued or as the emotion we experience on the way to reaching the goal. It's the goal itself or it's the goal-motivator. Experiencing happiness as a goal-driven motivator rather than pursuing it as the end-point is when happiness crosses over into joy.

According to the Centers for Disease Control and Prevention (CDC), about four out of ten Americans have not discovered a satisfying life purpose. Forty percent either do not think their lives have a clear sense of purpose or are neutral about whether their lives have purpose. Research has shown that having purpose and meaning in life increases overall well-being and life satisfaction, improves mental and physical health, enhances resiliency, enhances self-esteem, and decreases the chances of depression.

Many of us in the 21st century are organized around trying to be happy. Some would even say that we are obsessed by it. Just search amazon.com and count the number of books that have happiness in the title. "Happiness Coaches" are available in every city across the country to teach us how to be happier. The reason is evident—the scientific benefits linked to happiness are profound.

- Happy people have stronger, more intimate friendships.
- Happy people are more likely to be in satisfying romantic relationships.
- Happy people have a better functioning immune system.

- Happy people sleep better.
- Happy people are more creative.
- Happy people are more altruistic and generous.
- Happy people are viewed positively by other people. They are viewed as more likable, intelligent, physically attractive, confident, and have strong social skills.

A wide range of studies have demonstrated these positive outcomes. However, conditions such as the quantity and quality of our sleep, loneliness, and even making the pursuit of happiness our primary objective in life can negatively impact our happiness.

The dictionary definition of happiness is "a state of well-being, a pleasurable or satisfying experience." The definition of the word "rejoice," from which our word "joy" comes, is "to feel great delight, to welcome or to be glad." Depending on the translation, the Bible uses the words "happy" and "happiness" about 30 times, while "joy" and "rejoice" appear over 300 times. Many Christians hold the view that joy is NOT happiness. However, I believe that happiness and joy are facets of the same emotion. The difference is that happiness generally has an external cause. When circumstances are favorable or positive, we are naturally happy. But when events take a downward spiral, our spirits generally do so as well. Joy, on the other hand, has an internal cause and is not dependent upon circumstances. Those of us who are believers are content in good times and bad because our delight is in the Lord, not our fluctuating circumstances. Rick Warren puts it well when he says, "Joy is the settled assurance that God is in control of all the details of my life, the quiet confidence that ultimately everything is going to be all right, and the determined choice to praise God in every situation." Joy is not based on a *feeling*; it's based on *knowing*. For additional thoughts on joy, read Part II discussing joy as the second fruit of the Spirit.

Jesus used the word "blessed" in the Sermon on the Mount. It is from the Greek word *makarios*, which means to be happy or blissful, but it also means a self-contained happiness. The Greeks called the Island of Cypus "the happy isle." They believed that its geographical location, perfect climate, and fertile soil made it the ideal place to live. The term they associated with the island was *makarios*. They believed everything needed for happiness was right there on Cyprus.

We can't all move to Cyprus, but the idea is that **our happiness (joy) is independent of our circumstances.** It is self-contained, meaning that regardless of what is happening to us externally, we can be truly happy internally. We can choose an attitude of joyfulness because our life has meaning beyond the immediate situation.

Happiness impacts not only our emotional health but our physical health as well. When we bring things into our lives that create lasting joy, a very interesting physical response occurs. A gas called Nitric Oxide is released from the lining of our blood vessels. It is similar to the nitrous oxide that you may have received at the dentist. Dr. Ferid Murad won the 1998 Nobel Prize in Medicine for research leading to the discovery that Nitric Oxide is the body's signaling molecule.

Nitric Oxide is a very unstable free radical. It increases circulation as well as the production of neurotransmitters in the brain. Neurotransmitters are the chemical messengers that improve mood and help us deal with life's stresses. They also increase endorphins or the body's natural morphine which helps to dull pain and increase feelings of euphoria. Estrogen influences the process as well by binding to receptors in the lining of your blood vessels, and stimulating the release of Nitric Oxide, which in turn, causes our blood vessels to dilate. Can you see the amazing way that the spiritual, emotional, and physical all interrelate?

New science has shown us that when we view our stress as helpful, our blood vessels remain relaxed. Our heart may be pounding, preparing us for action, but there is no narrowing of our blood vessels. It resembles what happens to the body during times of joy or courage. Happiness and hope are key ingredients to a healthy stress response. In addition, when we are happy, another hormone called oxytocin—often referred to as the hormone of bonding—is also released. It is released when a woman nurses a baby, has an orgasm, or even when she gets together with good friends. Oxytocin is an anti-inflammatory neurohormone, which helps the body stay relaxed during times of stress. It acts on both the brain and the body to protect us from the cardiovascular effects of stress. Our heart has receptors for this hormone, and research demonstrates that it helps the heart cells to regenerate and heal from any stress-induced damage. So again we see the impact of happiness on not only our emotional health but our physical health.

The opposite of happiness includes emotions such as disappointment, discouragement, and depression. These emotions weigh us down like an anchor and rob us of happiness and the enjoyment (joy) of life because we become consumed with our circumstances. *Disappointment* comes when our expectations aren't met. We become unhappy when life doesn't turn out the way we envisioned it. Whether it's our marriage, pregnancy, children, job, or health, disappointment left unchecked leads to *discouragement* or losing courage. Living in the past or the future causes us to lose joy. Some people can't get over prior failures or mistakes while others fear what the future may hold. This type of thinking steals our contentment and joy "big time." We feel like we want to quit because we've become *disheartened.* We'd rather run away than deal with the situation. What follows discouragement is *depression.* It begins with *dejection* or a low spirit—a feeling of spiritual and emotional fatigue. Dejection can plunge us into *despair* which can end in feelings of complete *demoralization.* Hope is gone and replaced by apathy and numbness. Fear can also become overwhelming.

If we remain attentive in the present moment with our focus on the Lord, we will never lack reasons to rejoice. Recurring regrets can be silenced by accepting Christ's forgiveness and moving forward by His grace. The sin trap is to dwell on the "if onlys" and the "what ifs" of life. If we lose sight of Him and focus on our feelings or circumstances, our spirits will plummet and our joy will vanish like a puff of smoke. Fears are conquered by faith in God's promise to take care of our future. Jesus told his disciples, "So don't be anxious about tomorrow. God will take care of your tomorrow too. Live one day at a time." (Matthew 6:34 TLB). Not adding joy in our life leads to depression that cuts us off from seeing hope and purpose and what life and eternity are all about!

Happiness is a skill, just like any other skill that we learn and practice day by day such as golf or paddle boarding. It endures through the ups and downs of life. It is a way of interpreting the world. We may not be able to change the world but we can always change the way we look at it. The scientific understanding of happiness is currently being studied by researcher, Matt Killingsworth, a doctoral candidate from Harvard University. He found that staying in the moment is an important component to happiness. His study collected over 650,000 real-time reports from a globally diverse group of over 15,000 people with a wide range of income, age, and occupational status. The study showed that to really be happy, we must stay completely focused on our experience in the moment. On average, people are less happy when their minds are wandering. This was true even when they were doing a task that was not very enjoyable.

Cultivating happiness is different for everyone. It might be noticing sensations such as the smell of salt air or the feeling of a gentle breeze, or it may be getting together with friends, a good meal, or maybe even a massage or facial. It may be a more reflective process such as Biblical meditation and prayer, reading inspirational poetry or other readings, keeping a journal, or even buying fresh flowers, listening to your favorite music or simply enjoying a quiet moment. All these approaches are ways that can help to nourish your spirit and promote happiness.

Scientists have long known that there is a "pleasure center" or "reward center" in the brain. High concentrations of the neurotransmitter norepinephrine lead to feelings of extreme happiness while low levels have been linked to depression. This is the biological component of happiness. Effective coping strategies can improve a person's mood by increasing the amount of norepinephrine released in the brain. For example, **aerobic exercise, such as running, swimming, and brisk walking, can**

stimulate the release of norepinephrine by as much as four and a half times.

Set aside time each day to practice mindfulness and be attentive to present-moment experiences. Learn some relaxation techniques and use them. Turn off "cruise control" and really listen to others. Once we make a choice to practice mindfulness, God steps in to actively work on our behalf. The All-Powerful, Eternal, All-Knowing "shows Himself active on behalf of him who [earnestly] waits for Him," (Isaiah 64:4 AMP). The Lord Jesus said that "when He, the Spirit of Truth has come, He will guide you into all truth," (John 16:13). Devote your life to what matters. Put aside selfish interests and find meaning in Someone or something other than yourself. The Apostle Paul put it this way, "One thing I do, forgetting those things which are behind and reaching forward to those things which are ahead, I press toward the goal for the prize of the upward call of God in Christ Jesus. Therefore let us, as many as are mature, have this mind." (Philippians 3:13-15). This is *Your Mind Redefined.* For those of us who are believers in the Lord Jesus Christ, we have a God of HOPE and His hope fills us with joy and HAPPINESS.

PART II: READINGS TO RENEW YOUR MIND & RESTORE YOUR SPIRIT

"But the fruit of the Spirit is love, joy, peace, longsuffering, kindness, goodness, faithfulness, gentleness, self-control..."
-Galatians 5:22-23

INTRODUCTION: QUIET YOUR MIND & CULTIVATE THE FRUIT OF THE SPIRIT

The fruit of the Spirit must continually be cultivated in our minds. If we meditate on worries, anger, jealousies, lusts, fears, or grudges—toxic thoughts, we will reap selfish fruit in our behavior as well as our relationships. However, when we meditate on love, joy, peace, patience, kindness, goodness, faithfulness, gentleness, and self-control, we renew our minds and bear good fruit. The result is a strong and godly character.

Spend at least fifteen minutes every day prayerfully and meditatively reading the Scriptures and other inspirational sayings in each of the following chapters. Begin by sitting comfortably in a chair. Close your eyes and practice mindfulness breathing for about five minutes. Simply follow your breath and allow your whole body and mind to relax. Then select two or three entries on which to focus your attention. Meditate on the Scriptures and prayerfully consider what the words are saying and how they apply to your life. As you do, you will begin to renew your mind, get rid of toxic thoughts, and restore your spirit. Prayer is talking to God—meditation is God talking to you.

I urge you to keep a journal of how you can specifically apply these thoughts to areas of your life that need fertilizing, watering, pruning, and weeding. Be specific and list an action plan. You can use the *My Mindful Journal* to provide you with a structure to do this. By diligently tending your "garden," you will develop a godly character as the fruit of the Spirit mature in your life. While you are reading consider the following:

Am I harboring the poison of resentment, bitterness, or a grudge? Do I need to forgive myself or someone else? Do I need to seek forgiveness from someone? How has God shown His infinite mercy and grace to me? How can I show mercy and grace to someone else?

Am I thankful for everything—even if something doesn't turn out the way I had hoped? Do I remember to thank others on a regular basis?

What sin do I need to confess? Is it a sin of commission—i.e. jealousy, pride, addiction? Or is it a sin of omission—i.e. apathy, indifference, lack of commitment

Am I living in obedience to God's Word? What areas of my life are not aligned with Biblical principles? What areas of my life need "pruning" and "weeding?"

Am I living in the wisdom of Christ or do I seek to figure everything out myself? Remember Isaiah 55:8, "For My thoughts are not your thoughts, nor are your ways My ways, says the Lord."

As you renew your mind, your spirit will be restored and you will produce a harvest of fruit that will support optimal health. God is concerned with the attitudes of our hearts. II Corinthians 10:5 tells us to "bring every thought into captivity to the obedience of Christ." Only then will our minds be renewed and our spirits restored!

LOVE

"You shall love the Lord your God with all your heart, with all your soul, and with all your mind."
-Matthew 22:37

There are four kinds of love in the Bible—Eros, Agape, Philos, and Storje.

Eros is the name of the Greek god of love. Eros love is erotic love. This kind of love it associated with physical sensual love and is based on physical attraction. Erotic love is portrayed in the Old Testament book *The Song of Solomon* and is a necessary part of a healthy marriage.

Agape love is selfless, sacrificial, unconditional love—the highest of the four types of love in the Bible. Agape represents the divine love of God towards his Son Jesus Christ, human beings, and all believers. This love is the love that God commands all believers to have for everyone. It should never be determined by our feelings; it is more of a set of behaviors or actions. It is the love spoken about in the famous love chapter— I Corinthians 13. The Lord Jesus demonstrated agape by sacrificing himself for the sins of the world. "But God demonstrates His own love toward us, in that while we were still sinners, Christ died for us," (Romans 5:8). *In order to genuinely reflect love we need to receive God's love to us by faith. Once we are filled with God's love, we can begin loving ourselves, loving other people, and giving that love back to God in worship.*

Philos love is another kind of love—like the one we have for a companion or pal. Philia means close friendship or brotherly love in Greek. It refers to loving one another just like a close friend or family member. Romans 12:10 ESV instructs us to "Love one another with brotherly affection. Outdo one another in showing honor."

Storge is family love, the bond among mothers, fathers, sisters and brothers. Examples of family love that are found in Scripture include the love and mutual protection among Noah and his extended family, the love of Jacob for his sons, and the love that the sisters Martha and Mary had for their brother Lazarus.

The readings below all refer to some aspect of love—either God's love to us, our love to Him, or our love to other people around us. It begins with I Corinthians 13, which gives us a Biblical definition of love.

1 Corinthians 13:1-8a—*The Greatest Gift*

"Though I speak with the tongues of men and of angels, but have not love, I have become sounding brass or a clanging cymbal. And though I have the gift of prophecy, and understand all mysteries and all knowledge, and though I have all faith, so that I could remove mountains, but have not love, I am nothing. And though I bestow all my goods to feed the poor, and though I give my body to be burned, but have not love, it profits me nothing.

- Love suffers long and is kind;
- Love does not envy;
- Love does not parade itself, is not puffed up;
- Love does not behave rudely;
- Love does not seek its own;
- Love is not provoked;
- Love thinks no evil;
- Love does not rejoice in iniquity, but rejoices in the truth;
- Love bears all things;
- Love believes all things;
- Love hopes all things;
- Love endures all things;
- Love never fails."

"Therefore know that the Lord your God, He is God, the faithful God who keeps covenant and mercy for a thousand generations with those who love Him and keep His commandments," Deuteronomy 7:9.

"Oh, love the Lord, all you His saints! For the Lord preserves the faithful," Psalm 31:23.

"Therefore I love Your commandments more than gold, yes, than fine gold!" Psalm 119:127.

"Consider how I love Your precepts; Revive me, O Lord, according to Your lovingkindness," Psalm 119:159.

"Hatred stirs up strife, But love covers all sins," Proverbs 10:12.

"He who covers a transgression seeks love, But he who repeats a matter separates friends," Proverbs 17:9.

"So they come to you as people do, they sit before you as My people, and they hear your words, but they do not do them; for with their mouth they show much love, but their hearts pursue their own gain," Ezekiel 33:31.

"I drew them with gentle cords, with bands of love; and I was to them as those who take the yoke from their neck. I stooped and fed them," Hosea 11:4.

"He has shown you, O man, what is good; and what does the Lord require of you? But to do justly, to love mercy, and to walk humbly with your God," Micah 6:8.

"The Lord your God in your midst, The Mighty One, will save; He will rejoice over you with gladness, He will quiet you with His love, He will rejoice over you with singing," Zephaniah 3:17.

"Therefore love truth and peace." Zephaniah 8:19.

"He who loves father or mother more than Me is not worthy of Me. And he who loves son or daughter more than Me is not worthy of Me" Matthew 10:37—Jesus Christ

"Jesus said to him, You shall love the Lord your God with all your heart, with all your soul, and with all your mind. This is the first and great commandment. And the second is like it: 'You shall love your neighbor as yourself," Matthew 22:37-39.

"By this all will know that you are My disciples, if you have love for one another," John 13:35.

"If you love Me, keep My commandments," John 14:15 –Jesus Christ

"But God demonstrates His own love toward us, in that while we were still sinners, Christ died for us," Romans 5:8.

"Who shall separate us from the love of Christ? Shall tribulation, or distress, or persecution, or famine, or nakedness, or peril, or sword?" Romans 8:35.

"For I am persuaded that neither death nor life, nor angels nor principalities nor powers, nor things present nor things to come, nor height nor depth, nor any other created thing, shall be able to separate us from the love of God which is in Christ Jesus our Lord," Romans 8:38-39.

"To know the love of Christ which passes knowledge; that you may be filled with all the fullness of God," Ephesians 3:19.

"Speaking the truth in love," Ephesians 4:15.

"Walk in love, as Christ also has loved us and given Himself for us, an offering and a sacrifice to God for a sweet-smelling aroma," Ephesians 5:2.

"Husbands, love your wives, just as Christ also loved the church and gave Himself for her," Ephesians 5:25.

"That they admonish the young women to love their husbands, to love their children," Titus 2:4.

"For we have great joy and consolation in your love, because the hearts of the saints have been refreshed by you," Philemon 1:7.

"For God is not unjust to forget your work and labor of love which you have shown toward His name, in that you have ministered to the saints, and do minister," Hebrews 6:10.

"And above all things have fervent love for one another, for love will cover a multitude of sins," I Peter 4:8.

"Do not love the world or the things in the world. If anyone loves the world, the love of the Father is not in him," I John 2:15.

"But whoever has this world's goods, and sees his brother in need, and shuts up his heart from him, how does the love of God abide in him? My little children, let us not love in word or in tongue, but in deed and in truth," I John 3:17-18.

"There is no fear in love; but perfect love casts out fear, because fear involves torment. But he who fears has not been made perfect in love," I John 4:18.

"We love Him because He first loved us," I John 4:19.

"Immature love says: 'I love you because I need you.' Mature love says 'I need you because I love you.'"

--Erich Fromm

"Faith makes all things possible... love makes all things easy." –Dwight L. Moody

"Love cures people - both the ones who give it and the ones who receive it." –Karl A. Menninger

"Love is the beauty of the soul." –Saint Augustine

"Loving others always costs us something and requires effort. And you have to decide to do it on purpose. You can't wait for a feeling to motivate you." –Joyce Meyer

"Lord, grant that I might not so much seek to be loved as to love." – Francis of Assisi

O the Deep, Deep Love of Jesus

S. Trevor Francis 1834-1925

O the deep, deep love of Jesus, Vast, unmeasured, boundless, free;
Rolling as a mighty ocean, In its fullness over me.
Underneath me, all around me, Is the current of Thy love;
Leading onward, leading homeward! To my glorious rest above.

O the deep, deep love of Jesus, Spread His praise from shore to shore;
How He loveth, ever loveth, Changeth never, never more;
How He watches o'er His loved ones, Died to call them all His own;
How for them He intercedeth, Watcheth o'er them from the throne.

O the deep, deep love of Jesus, Love of ev'ry love the best;
'Tis an ocean vast of blessing, 'Tis a haven sweet of rest,
O the deep, deep love of Jesus, 'Tis a Heav'n of Heav'ns to me;
And it lifts me up to glory, For it lifts me up to Thee.

Questions to Ask Yourself:

1. How do I exhibit love in my daily life—towards God, my family, and others?
2. What prevents love from being exhibited in me? Have I personally experienced God's love to me through His Son? Do I regularly take the time to reflect on the vastness of His love?
3. What can I do to develop a more loving attitude toward others in my life even in times of disappointment, stress, or loneliness?
4. What steps do I need to take to put love into action in my marriage, family, at work, with friends, and to strangers? Do I need to confess an attitude of bitterness or lack of forgiveness? Does my own self-absorption get in the way of showing love? How can I apply love in my life to help me to endure suffering, setbacks, injury, sickness, or a death of a loved one?

JOY (GLADNESS, HAPPINESS)

"Do not sorrow, for the joy of the Lord is your strength."
-Nehemiah 8:10

Joy comes from the Greek word *chara*, meaning "to be exceedingly glad." The Bible uses the word joy (or rejoice) over 300 times. True joy is not dependent on external circumstances. James 1:2 says, "Consider it all joy, my brothers, when you encounter various trials." How could we ever consider going through difficulties and trials a reason to feel joy? James 1:3-4 gives us a clue when it says, "Knowing that the testing of our faith produces endurance. And let endurance have its perfect result, that you may be perfect and complete, lacking in nothing." The deep, abiding joy comes as we persevere through trials, with God's help, and our faith matures and is strengthened.

Life is hard—and some days it's difficult if not impossible to hold onto that feeling of joy. However, joy is not based on a *feeling*; it's based on *knowing*. It's true contentment and security that comes from internal factors like recognizing the sovereignty of God and that He is in control even when life seems to be turned upside down and inside out, (Psalm 32:7-9; James 1:2-4; I Peter 4:12-14)! He has saved us through Christ and has guaranteed our salvation through the Holy Spirit, (Ephesians 1:13-14). It's not about getting rid of our problems but getting rid of the FEAR of those problems.

These readings about joy refer to either God's joy toward us, the joy resulting from other people in our lives, or inward joy from applying God's principles to our lives. Our primary example of joy comes from observing our Savior, the Lord Jesus Christ. "Looking unto Jesus, the author and finisher of our faith, Who for the joy that was set before Him endured the cross, despising the shame, and has sat down at the right hand of the throne of God," (Hebrews 12:2). True joy is the result of knowing that everything we do has a purpose and is part of a divine plan. **We won't really know**

joy until we want God's will more than our own! Joy is the second fruit of the Spirit because we can't really know joy until we have grown and fertilized the first fruit of the Spirit—to know and love God.

"You will show me the path of life; In Your presence is fullness of joy; At Your right hand are pleasures forevermore," Psalm 16:11.

"I will offer sacrifices of joy in His tabernacle; I will sing, yes, I will sing praises to the Lord," Psalm 27:6.

"Weeping may endure for a night, But joy comes in the morning," Psalm 30:5.

"How joyful is the one whose transgression is forgiven, whose sin is covered!" Psalm 32:1.

"Restore to me the joy of Your salvation, And uphold me by Your generous Spirit," Psalm 51:12.

"Let us come before His presence with thanksgiving; Let us shout joyfully to Him with psalms," Psalm 95:2.

"Those who sow in tears shall reap in joy," Psalm 126:5.

"To console those who mourn in Zion, to give them beauty for ashes, the oil of joy for mourning, the garment of praise for the spirit of heaviness; That they may be called trees of righteousness, the planting of the Lord, that He may be glorified," Isaiah 61:3.

"Your words were found, and I ate them, and Your word was to me the joy and rejoicing of my heart; For I am called by Your name, O Lord God of hosts," Jeremiah 15:16.

"Yet I will rejoice in the Lord, I will joy in the God of my salvation," Habakkuk 3:18.

"Then the angel said to them, 'Do not be afraid, for behold, I bring you good tidings of great joy which will be to all people,'" Luke 2:10.

"Likewise, I say to you, there is joy in the presence of the angels of God over one sinner who repents," Luke 15:10.

"These things I have spoken to you, that My joy may remain in you, and that your joy may be full," John 15:11.

"Therefore you now have sorrow; but I will see you again and your heart will rejoice, and your joy no one will take from you," John 16:22.

"Until now you have asked nothing in My name. Ask, and you will receive, that your joy may be full,"

John 16:24.

"Now may the God of hope fill you with all joy and peace in believing, that you may abound in hope by the power of the Holy Spirit," Romans 15:13.

"For what is our hope, or joy, or crown of rejoicing? Is it not even you in the presence of our Lord Jesus Christ at His coming?" I Thessalonians 2:19.

"Yes, brother, let me have joy from you in the Lord; refresh my heart in the Lord," Philemon 1:20.

"Count it all joy when you fall into various trials," James 1:2.

"I have no greater joy than to hear that my children walk in truth," III John 1:4.

"Music... will help dissolve your perplexities and purify your character and sensibilities, and in time of care and sorrow, will keep a fountain of joy alive in you." — Dietrich Bonhoeffer

"My soul magnifies the Lord, And my spirit has rejoiced in God my Savior," — Mary (mother of Jesus) Luke 1:46-47

"Happiness, is not in another place, but this place . . . not for another hour, but for this hour." –Walt Whitman

"I have learned that in every circumstance that comes my way, I can choose to respond in one of two ways: I can whine or I can worship! And I can't worship without giving thanks. It just isn't possible. When we choose the pathway of worship and giving thanks, especially in the midst of difficult circumstances, there is a fragrance, a radiance that issues forth out of our lives to bless the Lord and others."
— Nancy Leigh DeMoss, *Choosing Gratitude: Your Journey to Joy*

". . .Find out where joy resides, and give it a voice far beyond singing. For to miss the joy is to miss all." –Robert Louis Stevenson

"When we are powerless to do a thing, it is a great joy that we can come and step inside the ability of Jesus" — Corrie ten Boom

Lord Jesus, Thou Who Only Art

Author Unknown

Lord Jesus, Thou who only art The endless source of purest joy,
O come and fill this longing heart; May nought but Thee my tho'ts employ.
Teach me on Thee to fix my eye, For none but Thee can satisfy.
The joys of earth can never fill The heart that's tasted of Thy love;
No portion would I seek until I reign with Thee, my Lord above,
When I shall gaze upon Thy face, And know more fully all Thy grace.
When from Thy radiant throne on high Thou didst my fall and ruin see,
Thou cam'st on earth for me to die, That I might share that throne with Thee.
Loved with an everlasting love, My hopes, my joys are all above.
O, what is all that earth can give? I'm called to share in God's own joy;
Dead to the world, in Thee I live, In Thee I've bliss without alloy:
Well may I earthly joys resign; All things are mine, and I am Thine!
Till Thou shalt come to take me home, Be this my one ambition, Lord,
Self, sin, the world, to overcome, Fast clinging to Thy faithful word;
More of Thyself each day to know, And more into Thine image grow.

Questions to Ask Yourself:

1. How do I exhibit joy in my daily life at home, at work, with others?
2. What gets in the way of joy being demonstrated in me—grief, stress, uncertainty?
3. Which of the "deadly D's" are preventing me from being able to "rejoice in the Lord," (Philippians 4:4)? – Disappointment – Discouragement – Disheartenment - Depression (dejection despair, and demoralization)
4. What steps do I need to take to put joy into action such as counteracting my attitude of self-pity or trying to manipulate my circumstances? How can I apply joy in my life to help me to endure suffering, setbacks, injury, sickness, or a death of a loved one?

PEACE

"You will keep him in perfect peace, whose mind is stayed on You, because he trusts in You."
-Isaiah 26:3

The peace or fellowship offering found in the Torah celebrated peace with God and was based on the sufficiency of the atoning blood. The person bringing this offering was expressing joyful gratitude for the peace resulting from fellowship with Jehovah. The peace offering might also be presented in connection with a vow to the Lord or in thanksgiving for some special favor. For the Christian, the peace offering symbolizes the finished work of Christ who made "peace through the blood of His cross," (Colossians 1:20).

"For Christ Himself has brought peace to us. He united Jews and Gentiles into one people when, in his own body on the cross, he broke down the wall of hostility that separated us. He did this by ending the system of law with its commandments and regulations. He made peace between Jews and Gentiles by creating in Himself one new people from the two groups. Together as one body, Christ reconciled both groups to God by means of his death on the cross, and our hostility toward each other was put to death," (Ephesians 2:14-16).

Let's keep our mind focused on the One Who can give us and keep us in perfect peace in a world filled with stress and turmoil. We either are trusting in ourselves and our own ingenuity and creativity to handle life's circumstances, or we are trusting in All-Powerful, All-Knowing, Eternal God of the universe Who knew us from our mother's womb and "*is acquainted with all of our ways*," (Psalm 139).

"The Lord lift up His countenance upon you, And give you peace,"

Numbers 6:26.

"And Mordecai sent letters to all the Jews, with words of peace and truth," Esther 9:30.

"I will both lie down in peace, and sleep; For You alone, O Lord, make me dwell in safety," Psalm 4:8.

"Depart from evil and do good; Seek peace and pursue it," Psalm 34:14.

"Great peace have those who love Your law, and nothing causes them to stumble," Psalm119:165.

"Deceit is in the heart of those who devise evil, but counselors of peace have joy," Proverbs 12:20.

"When a man's ways please the Lord, He makes even his enemies to be at peace with him," Proverbs 16:7.

"For unto us a Child is born, unto us a Son is given; And the government will be upon His shoulder. And His name will be called Wonderful, Counselor, Mighty God, Everlasting Father, Prince of Peace," Isaiah 9:6.

"Indeed it was for my own peace that I had great bitterness; But You have lovingly delivered my soul from the pit of corruption, for You have cast all my sins behind Your back," Isaiah 38:17.

"Oh, that you had heeded My commandments! Then your peace would have been like a river, And your righteousness like the waves of the sea," Isaiah 48:18.

"But He was wounded for our transgressions, He was bruised for our iniquities; The chastisement for our peace was upon Him, and by His stripes we are healed," Isaiah 53:5.

"For I know the thoughts that I think toward you, says the Lord, thoughts of peace and not of evil, to give you a future and a hope," Jeremiah 29:11.

"Salt is good, but if the salt loses its flavor, how will you season it? Have salt in yourselves, and have peace with one another," Mark 9:50.

"Peace I leave with you, My peace I give to you; not as the world gives do I give to you. Let not your heart be troubled, neither let it be afraid," John 14:27.

"These things I have spoken to you, that in Me you may have peace. In the world you will have tribulation; but be of good cheer, I have overcome the world," John 16:33.

"Therefore, having been justified by faith, we have peace with God through our Lord Jesus Christ," Romans 5:1.

"For to be carnally minded is death, but to be spiritually minded is life and peace," Romans 8:6

"Therefore let us pursue the things which make for peace and the things by which one may edify another," Romans 14:19.

"Now may the God of hope fill you with all joy and peace in believing, that you may abound in hope by the power of the Holy Spirit," Romans 15:13.

"And the God of peace will crush Satan under your feet shortly. The grace of our Lord Jesus Christ be with you. Amen," Romans 16:20.

"For God is not the author of confusion but of peace, as in all the churches of the saints," I Corinthians 14:33.

"And the peace of God, which surpasses all understanding, will guard your hearts and minds through Christ Jesus," Philippians 4:7.

"Now may the Lord of peace Himself give you peace always in every way. The Lord be with you all," II Thessalonians 3:16.

"Now no chastening seems to be joyful for the present, but painful; nevertheless, afterward it yields the peaceable fruit of righteousness to those who have been trained by it," Hebrews 12:11.

"Pursue peace with all people, and holiness, without which no one will see the Lord," Hebrews 12:14.

"Therefore, beloved, looking forward to these things, be diligent to be found by Him in peace, without spot and blameless," II Peter 3:14.

"Grace to you and peace from Him who is and who was and who is to come, and from the seven Spirits who are before His throne," Revelation 1:4.

"Restlessness and impatience change nothing except our peace and joy. Peace does not dwell in outward things, but in the heart prepared to wait trustfully and quietly on Him who has all things safely in His hands." — Elisabeth Elliot

"God cannot give us a happiness and peace apart from Himself, because it is not there. There is no such thing." – C. S. Lewis

"Peace is not merely a distant goal that we seek, but a means by which we arrive at that goal." ---Martin Luther King, Jr.

"We look forward to the time when the Power of Love will replace the

Love of Power. Then will our world know the blessings of peace." –William E. Gladstone

Oh, the Peace Forever Flowing

A.P. Cecil

Oh, the peace forever flowing From God's tho'ts of His own Son!
Oh, the peace of simply knowing On the cross that all was done!
Peace with God! The blood of heaven Speaks of pardon now to me:
Peace with God! The Lord is risen! Righteousness now counts me free.
Peace with God is Christ in glory; God is just and God is love;
Jesus died to tell the story, Foes to bring to God above.

Questions to Ask Yourself:

1. What signs and symptoms of inner peace do I see reflected in my life?
   - Have I lost interest in judging others?
   - Have I lost interest in judging myself?
   - Am I "delighting myself in the Lord" and seeking to enjoy each minute, (Psalm 37:4)?
   - Am I fretting or fearful about life's circumstances or do I commit my way to the Lord?
   - (I Peter 5:7)
   - Do I focus on things over which I have no control or have I learned to "rest in the Lord"?
   - Does guilt or shame about past experiences trouble me?
   - Do I let things happen rather than manipulate them and make them happen?
   - Do I get angry easily or I try to see circumstances through the "eyes" of others with flexibility and empathy?
   - Have I adopted an "attitude of gratitude" expressing frequent appreciation and thankfulness?
2. How has restlessness and impatience robbed me of peace?
3. What personal changes do I need to make in my life to experience peace of God?

PATIENCE (LONG-SUFFERING, EVEN-TEMPERED)

"But let patience have its perfect work, that you may be perfect and complete, lacking nothing."
-James 1:4

In the dictionary, the word patience has several meanings:

1. bearing pains or trials calmly and without complaining
2. not being hasty or impetuous
3. being steadfast despite opposition or adversity
4. showing forbearance under provocation or strain

We often think of patience (or being patient) as something passive such as the second meaning, but the dictionary definitions and the Bible imply that pain, trials, adversity, and stress may also be involved (James 1:2-4, 1 Peter 2:20, Romans 5:3-4, 12:12).

Patience can also be translated "even-tempered" or "long suffering." Does that sound like you? If not, take some time to *renew your mind* by cultivating this fruit of the Spirit. Patience is bound to hope, the hope that we have as believers as we anticipate the return of our Savior—"looking for the blessed hope and glorious appearing of our great God and Savior Jesus Christ," (Titus 2:13). We develop patience as we study the Scriptures and observe God's patience with His people through the years as well as their patience through the trials of life.

"And the Lord passed before him and proclaimed, 'The Lord, the Lord

God, merciful and gracious, longsuffering, and abounding in goodness and truth,'" Exodus 34:6.

"The Lord is longsuffering and abundant in mercy, forgiving iniquity and transgression; but He by no means clears the guilty, visiting the iniquity of the fathers on the children to the third and fourth generation," Numbers 14:18.

"He who has knowledge spares his words, and a man of understanding is of a calm spirit. Even a fool is counted wise when he holds his peace; When he shuts his lips, he is considered perceptive," Proverbs 17:27-28

"Count it all joy when you fall into various trials, knowing that the testing of your faith produces patience. But let patience have its perfect work, that you may be perfect and complete, lacking nothing," James 1:2-4.

"Such things were written in the Scriptures long ago to teach us. And the Scriptures give us hope and encouragement as we wait patiently for God's promises to be fulfilled," Romans 15:4 (NLT).

"That is why we are not discouraged. Though outwardly we are wearing out, inwardly we are renewed day by day," II Corinthians 4:16.

"Strengthened with all might, according to His glorious power, for all patience and longsuffering with joy," Colossians 1:11.

"The Lord is not slack concerning His promise, as some count slackness, but is longsuffering toward us, not willing that any should perish but that all should come to repentance," II Peter 3:9.

"Jesus knows the burdens we carry and the tears we shed. But He is the Healer of broken hearts, broken dreams, and broken lives. Trust Him. He never fails."—A Woman of Faith

"Patience is the companion of wisdom." –Saint Augustine

"Teach us, O Lord, the disciplines of patience, for to wait is often harder than to work." –Peter Marshall

"A wise man does not try to hurry history. Many wars have been avoided by patience, and many have been precipitated by reckless haste." Adlai Stevenson II

The Thorn

Martha Snell Nicholson

I stood a mendicant of God before His royal throne
And begged him for one priceless gift, which I could call my own.
I took the gift from out His hand, but as I would depart
I cried, "But Lord this is a thorn and it has pierced my heart.
This is a strange, a hurtful gift, which Thou hast given me."
He said, "My child, I give good gifts and gave My best to thee."
I took it home and though at first the cruel thorn hurt sore,
As long years passed I learned at last to love it more and more.
I learned He never gives a thorn without this added grace:
He takes the thorn to pin aside the veil which hides His face.

"Life's trials are not easy. But in God's will, each has a purpose. Often He uses them to enlarge you."—Warren Wiersbe

"He who bears failure with patience is as much of a philosopher as he who succeeds; for to put up with the world needs as much wisdom as to control it." –James H. Aughey

"The times we find ourselves having to wait on others may be the perfect opportunities to train ourselves to wait on the Lord." –Joni Eareckson Tada

"Now we exhort you, brethren, warn those who are unruly, comfort the fainthearted, uphold the weak, be patient with all," I Thessalonians 5:14.

Patience

Connie C. Bratcher

Oh, how we need patience
In our busy world today;
We have so many things to do
There's hardly time to pray.
Our calendars are so filled
That when we need to help a friend,
We find our patience running short-
Our schedules just won't bend.
Father, help us to be flexible,
And always follow Your lead,
As we help our friends
In their time of need.
We pray we'd have tender hearts
That truly understand,
Willing to go the extra mile
For our fellowman.
May our priorities always be
What You'd have them to be-
The needs of others first-
The things of eternity.
Give us empathy, and patience
That comes only from You,
And help us to be Christ-like
In everything we do.

Questions to Ask Yourself:

1. What are some situations in which I get frustrated and lose my patience?
2. What are the main differences in situations when I am patient and when I'm not patient?
3. The Bible frequently mentions a promise along with patience and perseverance (Psalm 37:7-9, 37:34, 40:1-3, Galatians 6:9, Hebrews 6:12, 10:36, James 5:7-8). What are these promises?
4. Does God have a reason to be impatient with me?
5. What "thorn" has God given me to teach me patience? How am I training myself to wait on the Lord?

KINDNESS

"She opens her mouth with wisdom, and on her tongue is the law of kindness."
-Proverbs 31:26

Kindness is the quality of being friendly, generous, and considerate. Helpfulness, thoughtfulness, unselfishness, hospitality, sympathy, and understanding all help to give us a picture of the word kindness. Are you unconditionally demonstrating the "law of kindness" to those around you? Every day you have a choice to speak words of kindness and demonstrate God's kindness through you. By making the right choice, you can brighten someone's life. The "law of kindness" is the gift that keeps on giving. . .

"And be kind to one another, tenderhearted, forgiving one another, even as God in Christ forgave you," Ephesians 4:32.

"To him who is afflicted, kindness should be shown by his friend, even though he forsakes the fear of the Almighty," Job 6:14.

"They refused to obey, and they were not mindful of Your wonders that You did among them. But they hardened their necks, and in their rebellion they appointed a leader to return to their bondage. But You are God, ready to pardon, gracious and merciful, slow to anger, abundant in kindness, and did not forsake them," Nehemiah 9:17.

"Because Your lovingkindness is better than life, my lips shall praise You," Psalm 63:3

"For his merciful kindness is great toward us: and the truth of the

LORD endureth forever. Praise ye the LORD," Psalm 117:2.

"What is desired in a man is kindness, and a poor man is better than a liar," Proverbs 19:22.

"Let, I pray, Your merciful kindness be for my comfort, according to Your word to Your servant," Psalm 119:76.

"But love your enemies, do good, and lend, hoping for nothing in return; and your reward will be great, and you will be sons of the Most High. For He is kind to the unthankful and evil," Luke 6:35.

"And the natives showed us unusual kindness; for they kindled a fire and made us all welcome, because of the rain that was falling and because of the cold," Acts 28:2.

"But love your enemies, do good, and lend, hoping for nothing in return; and your reward will be great, and you will be sons of the Most High. For He is kind to the unthankful and evil," Galatians 6:10.

"That in the ages to come He might show the exceeding riches of His grace in His kindness toward us in Christ Jesus. For by grace are ye saved through faith; and that not of yourselves: it is the gift of God: Not of works, lest any man should boast," Ephesians 2:7-9.

"Constant kindness can accomplish much. As the sun makes ice melt, kindness causes misunderstanding, mistrust, and hostility to evaporate."—Albert Schweitzer

"No matter how low down you are; no matter what your disposition has been; you may be low in your thoughts, words, and actions; you may be selfish; your heart may be overflowing with corruption and wickedness; yet Jesus will have compassion upon you. He will speak comforting words to you; not treat you coldly or spurn you, as perhaps those of earth would, but will speak tender words, and words of love and affection and kindness. Just come at once. He is a faithful friend – a friend that sticketh closer than a brother." – D.L. Moody

"No man can do me a truer kindness in this world than to pray for me." –Charles Spurgeon

"Kindness has converted more sinners than zeal, eloquence, or learning."—Frederick W. Faber

"You cannot do a kindness too soon because you never know how soon it will be too late." –Ralph Waldo Emerson

"I expect to pass through life but once. If therefore, there be any kindness I can show, or any good thing I can do to any fellow being, let me do it now, and not defer or neglect it, as I shall not pass this way again." – William Penn

"A kind heart is a fountain of gladness, making everything in its vicinity freshen into smiles,"–Washington Irving

"Kindness is more than deeds. It is an attitude, an expression, a look, a touch. It is anything that lifts another person," –Neil Strait

"Kindness is the language which the deaf can hear and the blind can see," --Mark Twain

"Am I as spontaneously kind to God as I used to be, or am I only expecting God to be kind to me? Am I full of the little things that cheer His heart over me, or am I whimpering because things are going hard with me? There is no joy in the soul that has forgotten what God prizes." — Oswald Chambers

The Little Things

Margaret Lindsey

The little things are most worthwhile--
A quiet word, a look, a smile,
A listening ear that's quick to share
Another's thoughts, another's care...
Though sometimes they may seem quite small,
These little things mean most of all.

Questions to Ask Yourself:

1. How do I exhibit kindness in my daily life at home, at work, with others?
2. What gets in the way of kindness being demonstrated in me—complacency, stress, bitterness?
3. How can I be a living example of God's kindness to others in my life? Be specific—my attitude, my facial expression, empathetic caring, praying for them.
4. Am I spontaneously kind to God, thinking about and doing the things that bring Him joy?
    - Uprightness of heart—being morally honorable, morally honest, respectable and to act righteously (I Chronicles 29:17)

- Magnifying the Lord and prospering/flourishing—growing spiritually (Psalm 35:27)
- A broken and contrite heart—having a humble repentant spirit for my sins arising from a pure love of God (Psalm 51:16-17)
- Praising Him in song and giving Him thanksgiving (Psalm 69:30-31)
- Reverencing Him and holding Him in awe (Psalm 147:10)
- Consistently telling the truth and being honest (Proverbs 12:22)
- Praying with fervency and reverence (Proverbs 15:8)
- Acting morally equitable to all, being humble and showing differential respect (Micah 6:7-8)
- Faith—diligently seeking Him (Hebrews 11:6)

GOODNESS (GENEROSITY)

"You are my Lord, My goodness is nothing apart from You."
-Psalm 16:2

The meaning of good or goodness often depends on how the word is used. Whether referring to a good book, a good friend, or good food, the common principle of goodness is that it provides some form of benefit, or fulfills its purpose or expectation. For people of faith, God is the One who defines moral goodness and sets the expectations that must be met. In fact, goodness is a quality of God that is so closely associated with Who He is, that people often use it as a euphemism for Him by saying "Oh my goodness!"

In Genesis 1 God referred to His creation as "good." It met His expectations and accomplished its purpose. This is the basic idea behind what the Spirit wants us to demonstrate in our lives—to meet God's expectations. Exodus 33:19 gives us God's response to Moses when he requested to see God's glory. The Lord says, "I will cause all my goodness to pass in front of you, and I will proclaim my name, the LORD [Yahweh], in your presence. I will have mercy on whom I will have mercy." God's goodness is expressed in merciful, gracious love which offers forgiveness and salvation to all who will receive it. Psalm 86:5 says, "For You, Lord, are good, and ready to forgive, and abundant in mercy to all those who call upon You." There is an overlapping of goodness with the other fruit of the Spirit such as kindness, gentleness, faithfulness, and love. Have you personally received God's goodness as demonstrated by His free gift of salvation? If so, are you reflecting His goodness, patience, forgiveness, and mercy to those around you?

"Surely goodness and mercy shall follow me All the days of my life; and I will dwell in the house of the Lord forever," Psalm 23:6.

"And the Lord passed before him and proclaimed, 'The Lord, the Lord God, merciful and gracious, longsuffering, and abounding in goodness and truth,'" Exodus 34:6.

"And they . . . delighted themselves in Your great goodness," Nehemiah 9:25.

"Oh, that men would give thanks to the Lord for His goodness, and for His wonderful works to the children of men!" Psalm 107:8.

"Do not remember the sins of my youth, nor my transgressions; According to Your mercy remember me, for Your goodness' sake, O Lord," Psalm 25:7.

"I would have lost heart, unless I had believed that I would see the goodness of the Lord in the land of the living," Psalm 27:13.

"Oh, how great is Your goodness, which You have laid up for those who fear You, which You have prepared for those who trust in You in the presence of the sons of men!" Psalm 31:19.

"For He satisfies the longing soul, and fills the hungry soul with goodness," Psalm 107:9.

"Most men will proclaim each his own goodness, but who can find a faithful man?" Proverbs 20:6.

"If a man begets a hundred children and lives many years, so that the days of his years are many, but his soul is not satisfied with goodness, or indeed he has no burial, I say that a stillborn child is better than he—," Ecclesiastes 6:3.

"Or do you despise the riches of His goodness, forbearance, and longsuffering, not knowing that the goodness of God leads you to repentance?" Romans 2:4.

"Therefore consider the goodness and severity of God: on those who fell, severity; but toward you, goodness, if you continue in His goodness. Otherwise you also will be cut off," Romans 11:22

"Therefore we also pray always for you that our God would count you worthy of this calling, and fulfill all the good pleasure of His goodness and the work of faith with power," II Thessalonians 1:11.

"Goodness is about character - integrity, honesty, kindness, generosity, moral courage, and the like. More than anything else, it is about how we treat other people." –Dennis Prager

"The great gift of Easter is hope - Christian hope which makes us have that confidence in God, in his ultimate triumph, and in his goodness and love, which nothing can shake." –Basil Hume

"Man has two great spiritual needs. One is for forgiveness. The other is for goodness." –Billy Graham

Your Goodness Overwhelms Me

Diane Christian

Your goodness overwhelms me
I can scarcely take it in
You broke my chains and freed me from sin
You showed me love and compassion
And pulled me out the deep dark pit
And in my life your light you lit
You made my darkens bright
And stood by me both day and night
You still loved me when I did things that I wanted to do
And now my life I give back to you
I am sorry for the times I may of had doubt
and my life with you I cannot be without

"Of all virtues and dignities of the mind, goodness is the greatest, being the character of the Deity; and without it, man is a busy, mischievous, wretched thing." –Francis Bacon

"Just as a mother finds pleasure in taking her little child on her lap, there to feed and caress him, in like manner our loving God shows His fondness for His beloved souls who have given themselves entirely to Him and have placed all their hope in His goodness." –Alphonsus Liguori

"Virtue is bold, and goodness never fearful." –William Shakespeare

"If you tell God no because He won't explain the reason He wants you to do something, you are actually hindering His blessing. But when you say yes to Him, all of heaven opens to pour out His goodness and reward your obedience. What matters more than material blessings are the things He is teaching us in our spirit." –Charles Stanley

The following hymn was found in A Collection of Hymns for the Use of the People Called Methodists, from the Bicentennial Edition of Wesley's Works. The Wesleys composed numerous hymns throughout their lifetime, but this one particularly stands out. It is the first hymn under the section entitled "*Describing the Goodness of God.*" Interestingly, the hymn does not talk about God's eternal attributes, His care of His creation, or even His care of us through the trials of life. Instead it launches right into a description of the cross. The hymn was written by Samuel Wesley, the father of Charles and John. Rather than beginning with a good God and theorizing about what that might mean, he starts at the cross and the atonement. By focusing our attention on the death of our Savior, we can more clearly understand that the cross is God's demonstration of His goodness to us.

Describing the Goodness of God

Samuel Wesley

Behold the Savior of mankind
Nailed to the shameful tree!
How vast the love that Him inclined
To bleed and die for thee!
Hark, how He groans, while nature shakes,
And earth's strong pillars bend;
The temple's veil in sunder breaks,
The solid marbles rend.
"'Tis done!" The precious ransom's paid,
"Receive My soul," He cries!
See where He bows His sacred head!
He bows His head, and dies!
But soon He'll break death's envious chain,
And in full glory shine:
O Lamb of God! was ever pain,
Was ever love, like Thine?

Questions to Ask Yourself:

1. Have I personally received God's goodness as demonstrated by His free gift of salvation?
2. How am I reflecting God's goodness, patience, forgiveness, and mercy to those around me? Give examples.
3. Do I agree with Billy Graham's quote: "Man has two great spiritual needs. One is for forgiveness. The other is for goodness,"? Why or why not?
4. How is the cross God's demonstration of His goodness to me?

FAITH (FAITHFULNESS)

"Through the Lord's mercies we are not consumed, because His compassions fail not. They are new every morning; great is Your faithfulness."
-Lamentations 3:22-23

The word faith is often used as a synonym for hope, trust, or belief. The Oxford Anglican theologian W. H. Griffith-Thomas states that faith is "not blind but intelligent. It commences with the conviction of the mind based on adequate evidence. . ." The New Testament uses the word faith over 240 times and is translated from the Greek word *pistis* which means assurance or to be persuaded. Faith must be evidence-based! Biblical faith causes personal change as it seeks a greater understanding of God, His character, and His plan for creation. As you meditate upon the following passages, **reflect upon the faithfulness of God and His requirements of faith in us.** Develop an action plan of how you can increase faith in your life and cause this fruit of the Spirit to grow and mature.

"Now faith is being sure of what we hope for and certain of what we do not see," Hebrews 11:1 (NIV).

"Looking unto Jesus, the author and finisher of our faith, who for the joy that was set before Him endured the cross, despising the shame, and has sat down at the right hand of the throne of God," Hebrews 12:2.

"Let us hold fast the confession of our hope without wavering, for He who promised is faithful," Hebrews 10:23.

"Therefore know that the Lord your God, He is God, the faithful God

RECOMMENDED SUPPLEMENTS

DAILY BEST ULTRA

Why take three pills a day when you can take just one? Our medical-grade vitamin/mineral provides all the foundational nutritional support you need. 26 nutrients provide support for brain health, heart health, eye health, bone health, fat metabolism, and proper glucose levels. No need to take extra Vitamin D (contains 2000 IU), zeaxanthin and lutein to help prevent macular degeneration and cataracts, and CoQ10 for cellular energy for heart, liver, and gums. Statin drugs and aging deplete your CoQ10 levels.

NONDAIRY PROBIOTIC 50

Support a healthy interaction between your gut microbes, your immune system and your brain. 90% of the body's serotonin and 50% of the body's dopamine is found in your "Abdominal Brain." Each vegetarian capsule is guaranteed to contain 52.5 billion CFUs of 9 species of micro-organisms including both lactobacillus and bifidobacterium to help you promote bowel function and ferment fiber. Normalize irritable bowel syndrome, Crohn's disease, ulcerative colitis, and celiac disease.

OMEGA-3 1000™

Help your brain cells to perform at peak levels by nourishing them with Essential Fatty Acids (EFA), a key component of our nerve cell membranes and important to communication between nerve cells. 99% of people in the U.S. do not eat sufficient omega-3 fatty acids. People with higher blood levels of DHA were less likely to show signs of dementia and had a larger hippocampus (memory portion of brain). Influences ADHD, Alzheimers, schizophrenia, bipolar, and depression.

ADRENAL BENEFITS

Is chronic stress causing you to feel "tired and wired" or fatigued and weary not relieved by sleep? Do you struggle to get through the day or are you driven and short-tempered with scattered thinking, anxiety, and an inability to focus? Regulate your adrenal hormone production, strengthen your memory, and promote clear thinking with Adrenal Benefits. Our unique blend of nutritional, botanical, and glandular factors will provide sustained energy without the roller coaster jitters of stimulants like caffeine.

RECOMMENDED SUPPLEMENTS

LIPOSOMAL MELATONIN SPRAY

Reset your sleep-wake cycle with our liposomal melatonin spray. Just 2 sprays on your tongue about one hour before your desired sleep time will boost melatonin without having to go through your digestive system. Convenient, easy to use, and fast-acting. A great option for jet lag and shift workers or simply to help you fall asleep and stay asleep naturally.

SERENITY NOW

When you need relief from symptoms of nervousness, irritability, frustration, low mood, and mental exhaustion during times of increased stress, chew one or two of our fast-acting, pleasant tasting orange/mint flavored tablets. The combination of Suntheanine® brand L-Theanine and Procalm™ brand Lactium, a patented bioactive peptide found in milk protein, work together to support the release of neurotransmitters in the brain to promote a more efficient calming response.

NEURO-DMG

An important supplement to support brain and neurological functions, Neuro-DMG helps reinforce your memory and recall, and promotes mental alertness, clear thinking, and reasoning. Our patented formula, DMG (Dimethylglycine HCL), helps to decrease symptoms associated with physical, emotional, and environmental stress by increasing circulation, oxygen utilization, mental alertness, and brain function. Support your brain with Neuro-DMG

B-12 MC SPRAY

With low levels prevalent in those over 60 years old, vitamin B-12 is essential to convert carbohydrates to glucose--our body's fuel. It also enables our body to convert fatty acids into energy and plays a key role in the production of melatonin—the sleep hormone. Common symptoms of low B-12 include: mental fatigue, low energy, mood changes, and sleep difficulties. Unlike pills which are poorly absorbed through the gut, our pre-metered non-aerosol spray is rapidly absorbed from your mouth.

who keeps covenant and mercy for a thousand generations with those who love Him and keep His commandments;" Deuteronomy 7:9.

"And the men did the work faithfully," II Chronicles 34:12.

". . .He was a faithful man and feared God more than many," Nehemiah 7:2.

"For there is no faithfulness in their mouth; Their inward part is destruction; Their throat is an open tomb; They flatter with their tongue," Psalm 5:9.

"Oh, love the Lord, all you His saints! For the Lord preserves the faithful. . ." Psalm 31:23.

"Your mercy, O Lord, is in the heavens; Your faithfulness reaches to the clouds," Psalm 36:5.

"And may not be like their fathers, a stubborn and rebellious generation, a generation that did not set its heart aright, and whose spirit was not faithful to God," Psalm 78:8.

"It is good to give thanks to the Lord, And to sing praises to Your name, O Most High; to declare Your lovingkindness in the morning, and Your faithfulness every night," Psalm 92:1-2.

"I know, O Lord, that Your judgments are right, and that in faithfulness You have afflicted me," Psalm 119:75.

"A talebearer reveals secrets, but he who is of a faithful spirit conceals a matter," Proverbs 11:13.

"A faithful witness does not lie, But a false witness will utter lies," Proverbs 14:5.

"Faithful are the wounds of a friend, But the kisses of an enemy are deceitful," Proverbs 27:6.

"O Lord, You are my God. I will exalt You, I will praise Your name, For You have done wonderful things; Your counsels of old are faithfulness and truth," Isaiah 25:1.

". . .And he who has My word, let him speak My word faithfully. . ." Jeremiah 23:28.

"O Ephraim, what shall I do to you? O Judah, what shall I do to you? For your faithfulness is like a morning cloud, And like the early dew it goes away," Hosea 6:4.

". . . The just shall live by his faith," Habakkuk 2:4.

"Now if God so clothes the grass of the field, which today is, and tomorrow is thrown into the oven, will He not much more clothe you, O you of little faith?" Matthew 6:30.

"But Jesus turned around, and when He saw her He said, 'Be of good cheer, daughter; your faith has made you well.' And the woman was made well from that hour," Matthew 9:22.

"For assuredly, I say to you, if you have faith as a mustard seed, you will say to this mountain, 'Move from here to there,' and it will move; and nothing will be impossible for you," Matthew 17:20.

"Woe to you, scribes and Pharisees, hypocrites! For you pay tithe of mint and anise and cummin, and have neglected the weightier matters of the law: justice and mercy and faith. These you ought to have done, without leaving the others undone," Matthew 23:23.

"His lord said to him, 'Well done, good and faithful servant; you were faithful over a few things, I will make you ruler over many things. Enter into the joy of your lord,'" Matthew 25:21.

"If then God so clothes the grass, which today is in the field and tomorrow is thrown into the oven, how much more will He clothe you, O you of little faith?" Luke 12:28.

"First, I thank my God through Jesus Christ for you all, that your faith is spoken of throughout the whole world," Romans 1:8.

"He did not waver at the promise of God through unbelief, but was strengthened in faith, giving glory to God," Romans 4:20.

"Therefore, having been justified by faith, we have peace with God through our Lord Jesus Christ," Romans 5:1.

"So then faith comes by hearing, and hearing by the word of God," Romans 10:17.

"Having then gifts differing according to the grace that is given to us, let us use them in proportion to our faith," Romans 12:6.

"God is faithful, by whom you were called into the fellowship of His Son, Jesus Christ our Lord," I Corinthians 1:9.

"That your faith should not be in the wisdom of men but in the power of God," I Corinthians 2:5.

"Moreover it is required in stewards that one be found faithful," I Corinthians 4:2.

"No temptation has overtaken you except such as is common to man;

but God is faithful, who will not allow you to be tempted beyond what you are able, but with the temptation will also make the way of escape, that you may be able to bear it," I Corinthians 10:13.

"Watch, stand fast in the faith, be brave, be strong," I Corinthians 16:13.

"For we walk by faith, not by sight," II Corinthians 5:7.

"I have been crucified with Christ; it is no longer I who live, but Christ lives in me; and the life which I now live in the flesh I live by faith in the Son of God, who loved me and gave Himself for me," Galatians 2:20.

"Therefore, as we have opportunity, let us do good to all, especially to those who are of the household of faith," Galatians 6:10.

"Above all, taking the shield of faith with which you will be able to quench all the fiery darts of the wicked one," Ephesians 6:16.

". . .Epaphras, our dear fellow servant, who is a faithful minister of Christ,. . ." Colossians 1:7.

". . .Rejoicing to see your good order and the steadfastness of your faith in Christ," Colossians 2:5.

"Remembering without ceasing your work of faith, labor of love, and patience of hope in our Lord Jesus Christ in the sight of our God and Father," I Thessalonians 1:3.

". . .Your faith toward God has gone out, so that we do not need to say anything," I Thessalonians 1:8.

"But let us who are of the day be sober, putting on the breastplate of faith and love, and as a helmet the hope of salvation," I Thessalonians 5:8.

"He who calls you is faithful, who also will do it," I Thessalonians 5:24.

"We are bound to thank God always for you, brethren, as it is fitting, because your faith grows exceedingly, and the love of every one of you all abounds toward each other," II Thessalonians 1:3.

"But the Lord is faithful, who will establish you and guard you from the evil one," II Thessalonians 3:3.

"Likewise, their wives must be reverent, not slanderers, temperate, faithful in all things," I Timothy 3:11.

"Let no one despise your youth, but be an example to the believers in word, in conduct, in love, in spirit, in faith, in purity," I Timothy 4:12.

"For the love of money is a root of all kinds of evil, for which some have strayed from the faith in their greediness, and pierced themselves through with many sorrows. But you, O man of God, flee these things and pursue righteousness, godliness, faith, love, patience, gentleness," I Timothy 6:10-11.

"If we are faithless, He remains faithful; He cannot deny Himself," II Timothy 2:13.

"And it was necessary for Jesus to be like us, his brothers, so that He could be our merciful and faithful High Priest before God, a Priest who would be both merciful to us and faithful to God in dealing with the sins of the people," Hebrews 2:17 (TLB).

"By faith we understand that the worlds were framed by the word of God, so that the things which are seen were not made of things which are visible," Hebrews 11:3.

"But without faith it is impossible to please Him, for he who comes to God must believe that He is, and that He is a rewarder of those who diligently seek Him," Hebrews 11:6.

"By faith Abraham obeyed when he was called to go out to the place which he would receive as an inheritance. And he went out, not knowing where he was going," Hebrews 11:8.

"By faith Sarah herself also received strength to conceive seed, and she bore a child when she was past the age, because she judged Him faithful who had promised," Hebrews 11:11.

"By faith Moses, when he became of age, refused to be called the son of Pharaoh's daughter," Hebrews 11:24.

"Knowing that the testing of your faith produces patience," James 1:3.

"But let him ask in faith, with no doubting, for he who doubts is like a wave of the sea driven and tossed by the wind," James 1:6.

"But someone will say, "You have faith, and I have works." Show me your faith without your works, and I will show you my faith by my works," James 2:18.

"Do you see that faith was working together with his works, and by works faith was made perfect?" James 2:22.

"That the genuineness of your faith, being much more precious than gold that perishes, though it is tested by fire, may be found to praise, honor, and glory at the revelation of Jesus Christ," I Peter 1:7.

"If we confess our sins, He is faithful and just to forgive us our sins and to cleanse us from all unrighteousness," I John 1:9.

"For whatever is born of God overcomes the world. And this is the victory that has overcome the world—our faith," I John 5:4.

". . .Be faithful until death, and I will give you the crown of life," Revelation 2:10.

"These will make war with the Lamb, and the Lamb will overcome them, for He is Lord of lords and King of kings; and those who are with Him are called, chosen, and faithful," Revelation 17:14.

"Faithless is he that says farewell when the road darkens." — J.R.R. Tolkien, *The Fellowship of the Ring*

"Faith is not the belief that God will do what you want. It is the belief that God will do what is right." — Max Lucado, *He Still Moves Stones*

"This is what the past is for! Every experience God gives us, every person He puts in our lives is the perfect preparation for the future that only He can see." — Corrie ten Boom, *The Hiding Place*

"Your children are the greatest gift God will give to you, and their souls the heaviest responsibility He will place in your hands. Take time with them, teach them to have faith in God. Be a person in whom they can have faith. When you are old, nothing else you've done will have mattered as much." — Lisa Wingate

"To one who has faith, no explanation is necessary. To one without faith, no explanation is possible." — Thomas Aquinas

"When all is said and done, the life of faith is nothing if not an unending struggle of the spirit with every available weapon against the flesh." — Dietrich Bonhoeffer, *The Cost of Discipleship*

"Everyone would like to have stronger faith. By themselves, the scriptures may not strengthen your faith, but being faithful to what they teach, does. In other words, faith cannot be separated from faithfulness." — John Bytheway, *When Times Are Tough: 5 Scriptures That Will Help You Get Through Almost Anything*

"It is this belief in a power larger than myself and other than myself which allows me to venture into the unknown and even the unknowable."— Maya Angelou

"Wait on the Lord" is a constant refrain in the Psalms, and it is a necessary word, for God often keeps us waiting. He is not in such a hurry as we are, and it is not his way to give more light on the future than we need for action in the present, or to guide us more than one step at a time. When in doubt, do nothing, but continue to wait on God. When action is needed, light will come." — J.I. Packer, *Knowing God*

"True faith rests upon the character of God and asks no further proof than the moral perfections of the One who cannot lie." — A.W. Tozer

My Faith Looks Up to Thee

Ray Palmer

My faith looks up to Thee, Thou Lamb of Calvary, Savior Divine!
Now hear me while I pray, Take all my guilt away, O let me from this day Be wholly Thine.
May Thy rich grace impart Strength to my fainting heart, My zeal inspire;
As Thou hast died for me, O may my love to Thee Pure, warm, and changeless be, A living fire!
While life's dark maze I tread And griefs around me spread, Be Thou my guide;
Bid darkness turn to day, Wipe sorrow's tears away, Nor let me ever stray From Thee aside.
When ends life's passing dream, When death's cold, threatening stream Shall o'er me roll,
Blest Savior, then, in love, Fear and distrust remove; O lift me safe above, A ransomed soul!

Questions to Ask Yourself:

1. What does it mean to live a life of faith?
2. How has God shown Himself to be faithful to me?
3. What do I currently have doubts about—my salvation, God's love for me, self-doubt, fundamental issues of the faith such as the reliability of Scripture, the reality of Hell, the exclusivity of Christ?
4. If true faith rests upon the character of God, what characteristics of God will help to strengthen my faith as I rest on Him?
5. How do trials test the genuineness of my faith?

GENTLENESS

"Let your gentleness be known to all men. The Lord is at hand."
-Philippians 4:5

The Apostle Paul wrote these words to the believers in Philippi, urging them to let others see their gentleness. But what did he mean by those words? According to William MacDonald, gentleness "has also been translated yieldedness, sweet reasonableness, and willingness to give up one's own way." Other synonyms for gentleness are sensitivity, tenderness, compassion, tolerance, and quietness. How do you "measure up?" It is one thing to understand what Paul is saying and another thing to obey this precept. Does everyone with whom you come in contact, including your family, see you as having a gentle spirit? The opposite of gentleness includes such characteristics as: abruptness, bitterness, cruelty, fury, aggressiveness, callousness, sternness, vengeance, revenge, and harshness.

Isaiah 42:3 clearly portrays the gentleness of the Messiah by the statement that He would not break a "bruised reed" or snuff out a "smoldering wick." Many people equate gentleness with weakness; however, this could not be further from the truth. In fact, I believe that the reverse is actually true. The Lord Jesus Christ drove the money changers out of the temple but at the same time described Himself as "gentle and humble in heart." Matthew 11:29. Strong individuals must learn to be gentle, to consciously bring their spirit into submission to God's Spirit and allow His fruit to mature in their lives. This is an ongoing process, and can become very frustrating. However, a gentle person still speaks the truth but has learned to do so in way that it can be received by modifying their choice of words and tone of voice. For more pointers on communication, re-read the chapter on Five Keys to Developing Your Emotional Health. As you read the following scriptures and quotations, meditate on those areas of your life that need to be conformed to the image of Christ so that His gentleness will be reflected in you. We need to be transformed, "by the renewing of our mind," Romans 12:2. The reason—"The Lord is at hand."

"To speak evil of no one, to avoid quarreling, to be gentle, and to show perfect courtesy toward all people," Titus 3:2 ESV.

"But in your hearts honor Christ the Lord as holy, always being prepared to make a defense to anyone who asks you for a reason for the hope that is in you; yet do it with gentleness and respect," I Peter 3:15 ESV.

"You have given me the shield of Your salvation; Your right hand has held me up, Your gentleness has made me great," Psalm 18:35.

"And a servant of the Lord must not quarrel but be gentle to all, able to teach, patient, in humility correcting those who are in opposition, if God perhaps will grant them repentance, so that they may know the truth," II Timothy 2:24-25.

"But the wisdom that is from above is first pure, then peaceable, gentle, willing to yield, full of mercy and good fruits, without partiality and without hypocrisy," James 3:17.

"Brethren, if a man is overtaken in any trespass, you who are spiritual restore such a one in a spirit of gentleness, considering yourself lest you also be tempted," Galatians 6:1.

"Take My yoke upon you and learn from Me, for I am gentle and lowly in heart, and you will find rest for your souls," –Lord Jesus Christ Matthew 11:29.

"A soft answer turns away wrath, but a harsh word stirs up anger," Proverbs 15:1.

"With all lowliness and gentleness, with longsuffering, bearing with one another in love," Ephesians 4:2.

"So then, my beloved brethren, let every man be swift to hear, slow to speak, slow to wrath; for the wrath of man does not produce the righteousness of God," James 1:19-20.

"But we were gentle among you, just as a nursing mother cherishes her own children," I Thessalonians 2:7.

"But you, O man of God, . . . pursue righteousness, godliness, faith, love, patience, gentleness," I Timothy 6:11.

"Only the weak are cruel. Gentleness can only be expected from the strong." –Leo Buscaglia

"A Christian reveals true humility by showing the gentleness of Christ, by being always ready to help others, by speaking kind words and performing unselfish acts, which elevate and ennoble the most sacred message that has come to our world." –Ellen G. White

"When you encounter difficulties and contradictions, do not try to break them, but bend them with gentleness and time." –Saint Francis de Sales

"I choose gentleness... Nothing is won by force. I choose to be gentle. If I raise my voice may it be only in praise. If I clench my fist, may it be only in prayer. If I make a demand, may it be only of myself." -Max Lucado

"It's the hard things that break; soft things don't break. It was an epiphany I had today and I just wonder why it took me so very, very long to see it! You can waste so many years of your life trying to become something hard in order not to break; but it's the soft things that can't break! The hard things are the ones that shatter into a million pieces!" — C. JoyBell C.

"Gentleness is not apathy but is an aggressive expression of how we view people. We see people as so valuable that we deal with them in gentleness, fearing the slightest damage to one for whom Christ died. To be apathetic is to turn people over to mean and destructive elements, to truly love people cause for us to be aggressively gentle." — Gayle D. Erwin, *Spirit Style*

I Greet Thee Who My Sure Redeemer Art

Attributed to: John Calvin

I greet Thee, who my sure Redeemer art,
My only trust and Savior of my heart,
Who pain didst undergo for my poor sake;
I pray Thee from our hearts all cares to take.

Thou hast the true and perfect gentleness,
No harshness hast Thou and no bitterness;
Make us to taste the sweet grace found in Thee
And ever stay in Thy sweet unity.

Questions to Ask Yourself:

1. How have I demonstrated that I am willing to give up my own way and yield to others in my life?
2. Am I tolerant to those with a different culture or viewpoint from my own? Do I communicate with respect? Do I uphold Scriptural principles presenting them with gentleness without being degrading

or demanding?

3. Do I really listen empathically to others without thinking about what I am going to say next? Can I communicate without raising my voice in anger or frustration?
4. What does it mean to be aggressively gentle?
5. What can I learn from Christ's gentleness that I can apply to my own life?

SELF-CONTROL

"Giving all diligence, add to your faith virtue, to virtue knowledge, and to knowledge self-control, to self-control perseverance, to perseverance godliness."
-II Peter 1:5-6

The word self-control appears only four times in the New Testament and two of those times are in the verses listed above. Different versions of the Bible translate the word as self-restraint, chastity, temperance, or continence. Self-control is the ability to control our emotions, speech, behaviors, and desires by bringing "every thought into captivity to the obedience of Christ." (II Corinthians 10:5). So the fruit of "self-control" is really "Spirit-controlled." Are your emotions, speech, behaviors, or desires out of control or are they being guided by the Holy Spirit? Anger, anxiety, jealousy, gossiping, lust, vulgar language, addictions, and poor time management are just a few examples of not allowing the fruit of "self-control" to blossom in your life.

A study done at the University of Pennsylvania surveyed two million people and asked them to rank order their strengths in 24 different skills. Guess what skill ended up in the very bottom? If you said self-control you are correct! Some of the reason is that self-control is part of a success/failure cycle. Our desires can become temptations when they conflict with our values. Self-control is a key element in this process.

Here are six important strategies to help us to increase our self-control:

1. **Meditation or Mindfulness:** That's what Part II of this book is all about. By taking as little as ten to twenty minutes per day to focus on our breathing and our senses, we will improve our self-awareness and our brain's ability to resist destructive impulses. If we bring our thoughts into alignment with spiritual principles it will increase our success rate. Simply follow your breath and allow your whole body and mind to relax for about five minutes. Then select

two or three entries on which to focus your attention. Meditate on the Scriptures and prayerfully consider what the words are saying and how they apply to your life. As you do, you will begin to renew your mind, get rid of toxic thoughts, and restore your spirit. Journal your insights to strengthen the connection between your desires and values and thus increase your self-control. Use the *My Mindful Journal* to provide a daily structure for your journaling.

2. **Eat:** When we are attempting to exert self-control, our brain causes the body to burn our stores of glucose, decreasing blood sugar while at the same time increasing our destructive impulses. If we reach for a candy bar, our blood sugar levels will spike quickly and then leave us drained and vulnerable. Eating something that will provide a slower energy source such as whole wheat or rice crackers with cheese or other protein will give us more fuel for self-control.
3. **Exercise:** After only ten minutes of exercise, a neurotransmitter called GABA is released. GABA helps your brain to feel soothed and keeps your impulses under control. If you feel like you're going to explode in a fit of anger, walk away and keep walking for a few minutes. By the time you return, your self-control "switch" should be reset.
4. **Sleep:** Our brain cell's ability to absorb glucose is diminished when we're tired. Getting a good night's sleep is essential to provide the glucose needed to help control our impulses. In addition, without enough sleep we're more likely to crave sugary snacks to compensate for low glucose levels.
5. **Wait:** If you have a strong desire or urge, wait at least ten minutes before acting on it. Desire has a tendency to ebb and flow like a tide. Chances are that after about ten minutes, the wave of desire will become only a small ripple that we can easily manage.
6. **Forgive yourself:** When you slip up, don't keep wallowing in the problem. See the situation from God's perspective and seek His forgiveness. Ask for forgiveness from whoever was impacted by your lack of self-control. Then forgive yourself and move on. Focus on what to do differently in the future.

As you consider the following passages, develop a specific action plan to prune the weeds of worry, anger, bad language, jealousy, lust or other areas which are choking out the fruit of self-control. The passages contain examples to follow as well as examples not to follow. Set goals that will bring your desires in harmony with your values. Colossians 3: 1-4 gives us the pattern: "If then you were raised with Christ, seek those things which are above, where Christ is, sitting at the right hand of God. Set your mind on things above, not on things on the earth. For you died, and your life is hidden with Christ in God. When Christ who is our life appears, then you also will appear with Him in glory." Don't follow Felix's example listed below and wait for a more convenient time. Make self-control your priority!

"Now as he (Paul) reasoned about righteousness, self-control, and the judgment to come, Felix was afraid and answered, "Go away for now; when I have a convenient time I will call for you," Acts 24:25.

Anger

"Be angry, and do not sin: do not let the sun go down on your wrath," Ephesians 4:26.

"So Moses' anger became hot, and he cast the tablets out of his hands and broke them at the foot of the mountain," Exodus 32:19.

"The Lord is gracious and full of compassion, slow to anger and great in mercy," Psalm 145:8.

"A soft answer turns away wrath, but a harsh word stirs up anger," Proverbs 15:1.

"The discretion of a man makes him slow to anger, and his glory is to overlook a transgression," Proverbs 19:11.

"A gift in secret pacifies anger, and a bribe behind the back, strong wrath," Proverbs 21:14.

"Do not hasten in your spirit to be angry, for anger rests in the bosom of fools," Ecclesiastes 7:9.

"Let all bitterness, wrath, anger, clamor, and evil speaking be put away from you, with all malice, and be kind to one another, tenderhearted, forgiving one another, even as God in Christ forgave you." Ephesians 4:31-32.

Anxiety

"Anxiety in the heart of man causes depression, but a good word makes it glad," Proverbs 12:25.

"Casting all your care upon Him, for He cares for you," I Peter 5:7.

"There is no fear in love; but perfect love casts out fear, because fear involves torment. But he who fears has not been made perfect in love," I John 4:18.

"And the Lord, He is the One who goes before you. He will be with you, He will not leave you nor forsake you; do not fear nor be dismayed,"

Deuteronomy 31:8.

"The Lord is my light and my salvation; Whom shall I fear? The Lord is the strength of my life; of whom shall I be afraid?" Psalm 27:1.

"In the multitude of my anxieties within me, Your comforts delight my soul," Psalm 94:19.

Jealousy

"Wrath is cruel and anger a torrent, But who is able to stand before jealousy?" Proverbs 27:4.

"A relaxed attitude lengthens a man's life; jealousy rots it away," Proverbs 14:30 (TLB).

"Do not let your heart envy sinners, but be zealous for the fear of the Lord all the day;" Proverbs 23:17.

"Love does not envy;" I Corinthians 13:4.

"Incline my heart to Your testimonies, and not to covetousness," Psalm 119:36.

Gossiping

". . .A whisperer separates the best of friends," Proverbs 16:28.

"They learn to be idle, wandering about from house to house, and not only idle but also gossips and busybodies, saying things which they ought not," I Timothy 5:13.

"Set a guard, O Lord, over my mouth; keep watch over the door of my lips," Psalm 141:3.

Lust/Sexuality

"For all that is in the world—the lust of the flesh, the lust of the eyes, and the pride of life—is not of the Father but is of the world," I John 2:16.

"Do not deprive one another except with consent for a time, that you may give yourselves to fasting and prayer; and come together again so that Satan does not tempt you because of your lack of self-control," I Corinthians 7:5 (*Speaking about husbands and wives*).

"But if they cannot exercise self-control, let them marry. For it is better to marry than to burn with passion," I Corinthians 7:9.

"As soon as her eyes saw them, (Clothed most gorgeously, horsemen riding on horses, all of them desirable young men), she lusted for them and sent messengers to them," Ezekiel 23:12,16.

"But I (Jesus) say to you that whoever looks at a woman to lust for her has already committed adultery with her in his heart," Matthew 5:28.

"Likewise also the men, leaving the natural use of the woman, burned in their lust for one another, men with men committing what is shameful, and receiving in themselves the penalty of their error which was due," Romans 1:27.

"Therefore do not let sin reign in your mortal body, that you should obey it in its lusts," Romans 6:12.

"But put on the Lord Jesus Christ, and make no provision for the flesh, to fulfill its lusts," Romans 13:14.

"Walk in the Spirit, and you shall not fulfill the lust of the flesh," Galatians 5:16.

"Flee also youthful lusts; but pursue righteousness, faith, love, peace with those who call on the Lord out of a pure heart," II Timothy 2:22.

"Teaching us that, denying ungodliness and worldly lusts, we should live soberly, righteously, and godly in the present age," Titus 2:12.

"As obedient children, not conforming yourselves to the former lusts, as in your ignorance;" I Peter 1:14.

"Beloved, I beg you as sojourners and pilgrims, abstain from fleshly lusts which war against the soul," I Peter 2:11.

Speech

"But now you yourselves are to put off all these: anger, wrath, malice, blasphemy, filthy language out of your mouth," Colossians 3:8.

"Keep your tongue from evil, and your lips from speaking deceit," Psalm 34:13.

"And my tongue shall speak of Your righteousness And of Your praise all the day long," Psalm 35:28.

"I will bless the Lord at all times; His praise shall continually be in my mouth," Psalm 34:1.

"The mouth of the righteous speaks wisdom, and his tongue talks of justice," Psalm 37:30.

"I will guard my ways, lest I sin with my tongue; I will restrain my mouth with a muzzle, while the wicked are before me," Psalm 39:1.

"Deliver my soul, O Lord, from lying lips and from a deceitful tongue," Psalm 120:2.

"For there is not a word on my tongue, but behold, O Lord, You know it altogether," Psalm 139:4.

"The tongue of the righteous is choice silver;" Proverbs 10:20.

"There is one who speaks like the piercings of a sword, but the tongue of the wise promotes health," Proverbs 12:18.

"The truthful lip shall be established forever, but a lying tongue is but for a moment," Proverbs 12:19.

"A wholesome tongue is a tree of life, But perverseness in it breaks the spirit," Proverbs 15:4.

"A gentle tongue breaks a bone," Proverbs 25:15.

"A backbiting tongue (brings forth) an angry countenance," Proverbs 25:23.

"She opens her mouth with wisdom, and on her tongue is the law of kindness," Proverbs 31:26.

Addictions

"Do not join those who drink too much wine or gorge themselves on meat," Proverbs 23:20 (NIV).

"Woe to those who rise early in the morning, that they may follow intoxicating drink; who continue until night, till wine inflames them!" Isaiah 5:11.

"Wine is a mocker, strong drink is a brawler, and whoever is led astray by it is not wise," Proverbs 20:1.

"For the drunkard and the glutton will come to poverty" Proverbs 23:21.

"But they also have erred through wine, and through intoxicating drink are out of the way; The priest and the prophet have erred through intoxicating drink, they are swallowed up by wine, they are out of the way through intoxicating drink; They err in vision, they stumble in judgment," Isaiah 28:7.

"It is good neither to eat meat nor drink wine nor do anything by which your brother stumbles or is offended or is made weak," Romans 14:21.

"Do not get drunk on wine, which leads to debauchery (excessive indulgence in lust or sensuality). Instead, be filled with the Spirit," Ephesians 5:18.

"The older women likewise, that they be reverent in behavior, not slanderers, not given to much wine, teachers of good things," Titus 2:3.

Time Management

"To everything there is a season, A time for every purpose under heaven: A time to be born, and a time to die; A time to plant, and a time to pluck what is planted; A time to kill, and a time to heal; A time to break down, and a time to build up; ..." Ecclesiastes 3:1-3.

"Six days you shall work, but on the seventh day you shall rest; in plowing time and in harvest you shall rest," Exodus 34:21.

"See then that you walk circumspectly, not as fools but as wise, redeeming the time, because the days are evil," Ephesians 5:15-16.

"For in the time of trouble He shall hide me in His pavilion; In the secret place of His tabernacle He shall hide me; He shall set me high upon a rock," Psalm 27:5.

"My times are in Your hand," Psalm 31:15.

"Trust in Him at all times, you people; Pour out your heart before Him; God is a refuge for us," Psalm 62:8.

"Behold, now is the accepted time; behold, now is the day of salvation," II Corinthians 6:2.

"Walk in wisdom toward those who are outside, redeeming the time," Colossians 4:5.

"You do not know what will happen tomorrow. For what is your life? It is even a vapor that appears for a little time and then vanishes away," James 4:14.

"That he no longer should live the rest of his time in the flesh for the lusts of men, but for the will of God," I Peter 4:2.

"The time has come for you to reap, for the harvest of the earth is ripe," Revelation 14:15.

"People often complain about lack of time when the lack of direction is the real problem." –Zig Ziglar

"The most efficient way to live reasonably is every morning to make a plan of one's day and every night to examine the results obtained." –Alexis

Carrel

All for Jesus

Mary D. James

All for Jesus! All for Jesus!
All my being's ransomed pow'rs;
All my thoughts and words and doings,
All my days and all my hours.
All for Jesus! All for Jesus!
All my days and all my hours.
All for Jesus! All for Jesus!
All my days and all my hours.

Let my hands perform His bidding;
Let my feet run in His ways;
Let mine eyes see Jesus only;
Let my lips speak forth His praise.
All for Jesus! All for Jesus!
Let my lips speak forth His praise.
All for Jesus! All for Jesus!
Let my lips speak forth His praise.

Since mine eyes were fixed on Jesus,
I've lost sight of all beside—
So enchained my spirit's vision,
Looking at the Crucified.
All for Jesus! All for Jesus!
Looking at the Crucified.
All for Jesus! All for Jesus!
Looking at the Crucified.

Oh, what wonder! how amazing!
Jesus, glorious King of kings,
Deigns to call me His beloved,
Lets me rest beneath His wings.
All for Jesus! All for Jesus!
Resting now beneath His wings.
All for Jesus! All for Jesus!
Resting now beneath His wings.

"I beseech you therefore, brethren, by the mercies of God, that you present your bodies a living sacrifice, holy, acceptable to God, which is your reasonable service. And do not be conformed to this world, but **be transformed by the renewing of your mind,** that you may prove what is that good and acceptable and perfect will of God," Romans 12:1-2. Take control of your thoughts and reach your optimal health!

Questions to Ask Yourself:

1. Which areas of self-control do I have the most trouble with—eating, anger, anxiety, jealousy, gossiping, lust, vulgar language, addictions, time management? Why? Has this changed over time?
2. What are the triggers that prevent me from maintaining my self-control?
3. If I realize that I am going to be in a situation that requires self-control, how do I try to prepare myself ahead of time? Do I try to avoid the situation?
4. If I've lost my self-control do I try to determine what I will do differently next time?
5. What relaxation strategies do I routinely practice—relaxation breathing, progressive muscle relaxation, journaling, mindfulness, exercise, prayer and Bible reading?
6. Do I think that God is willing to help me with self-control, (Galatians 5:16, I Corinthians 10:13, James 4:7-8)? How is the Holy Spirit helping me to cultivate the fruit of self-control? Be specific.

PRESS ON TOWARDS THE GOAL

"One thing I do, forgetting those things which are behind and reaching forward to those things which are ahead, I press toward the goal for the prize of the upward call of God in Christ Jesus,"
-Philippians 3:13-14

Now that you've rediscovered God's plan for health, hope, and happiness you may be wondering how to integrate all this information about brain strain, relaxation techniques, lifestyle choices, and spiritual growth into your daily life? It can seem like a daunting task! The starting point is simply understanding the intricate way that God has caused our body, mind, and spirit to work together to promote health and wellness. It removes any shame, self-blame, and stigma that so often accompanies emotional problems and gives you the freedom to "press on."

Look for progress not perfection. Are you learning how to quiet your mind and cultivate the fruit of the Spirit? What "weeds" have you needed to uproot—resentment, bitterness, lack of forgiveness, apathy, pride? What areas have needed "pruning"—time management, anxious thoughts, eating and exercise habits? Are you "fertilizing" your brain with BDNF, that wonderful protein, by keeping your stress under control and doing thirty minutes of aerobic exercise at least five times per week?

Consider developing the habit of daily journaling using the *My Mindful Journal*. Mindful writing is a valuable tool for personal reflection and perspective. It allows us to process emotional experiences when we are better able to think about them on a conscious level. Self-awareness is the first skill to understand our emotions and how they influence our behaviors. Take yourself off auto-pilot or cruise control and allow things to slow down. From ancient times the Bible has stressed the importance of being quiet and waiting on God. The Psalmist tells us, "Surely I have calmed and quieted my soul," (Psalm 131:2). The initiative begins with us. We need to find a special place where we can be alone with God every day—away from the distractions of the Internet, television, cell phones and even other family members. Once we make a conscious choice to practice mindfulness, God steps in to actively work on our behalf. The all-powerful, eternal, all-knowing God "shows Himself active on behalf of him who [earnestly] waits for Him," (Isaiah 64:4 AMP).

The choice is yours. The effects of your daily choices accumulate and will either result in chronic debilitating illness or a vibrant balanced life. Let God redefine your mind!

APPENDIX I: PROGESTERONE CREAM APPLICATION

I recommend using a pharmaceutical-grade 1.6% - 3% progesterone cream of 450 - 500 mg. progesterone per ounce. This concentration is very low and should not present any problems for most women.

Always consult your healthcare provider before starting any type of hormone replacement. It is essential to obtain some baseline tests including a pelvic ultrasound to measure your uterine lining and a complete physical including a GYN check-up, breast exam, pap smear and mammogram (if over 40 years old). A 24-hour urine test is the most accurate way to test your hormone levels. If you plan to take both estrogen and progesterone, start with only estrogen for a few days to a week in order to get your estrogen balanced.

The best approach is to apply progesterone cream in a divided dose with a larger dose at bedtime to help promote normal sleep patterns. Use it after showering for better absorption. Apply 1/16 to 1/4 teaspoon of the cream to areas of thinner skin such as the inner arms or thighs, or where you blush such as your neck, chest, or face. Rotate areas to avoid saturation. It is important to recognize signs of excess progesterone replacement and adjust the dosage accordingly.

Reactions usually occur within a half hour of taking the hormone and can last from two hours to up to eight hours in cases of severe reactions. Mild reactions can include drowsiness, slight dizziness, and a sense of physical instability. Signs and symptoms of a more severe reaction can be a feeling of being drunk or spinning and heaviness of your arms and legs.

There is also a reaction called a paradoxical response. Some women can only tolerate a minimum amount of extra progesterone. One of my patients reported a reaction after using only 1/16 of a teaspoon of a 2% cream. That is why it's important to work closely with your healthcare provider to determine the appropriate dose you need to achieve benefit. The three types of paradoxical responses include:

- Feeling anxious, difficulty sleeping and retaining fluid. This response is possibly due to progesterone converting to cortisol, the stress hormone. Progesterone may also convert to deoxycorticosterone, a hormone that regulates fluid balance.
- Hot flashes or depression—Progesterone overloads the estrogen receptors at the cellular level causing less estrogen to be available to the cells. Signs of estrogen deficiency, such as hot flashes and depression, then develop. Contact your healthcare provider to reduce the progesterone dose if this occurs.
- Increased appetite and weight gain—This happens only occasionally and there is no scientific explanation.

APPENDIX II: CORTISOL CONTROLLED BY THE HPA AXIS - A NEGATIVE FEEDBACK LOOP

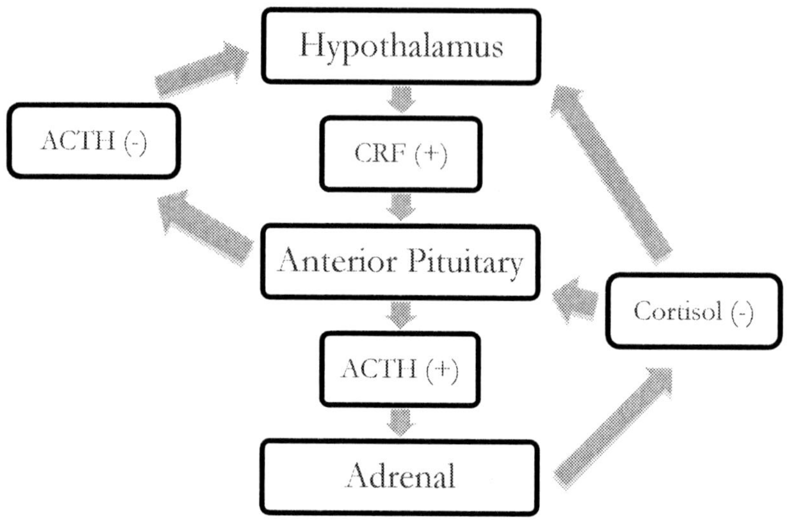

Cortisol: Referred to as the "stress hormone". It preps us for action by stimulating norepinephrine to flip the switch on our fight/flight response. Chronic stress and prolonged cortisol secretion can cause high blood pressure, atherosclerosis, diabetes, a weakened immune system, muscle atrophy, and osteoporosis.

Negative Feedback Loop: This is a cortisol checks-and-balance system. The HPA axis adjusts cortisol levels according to the body's need. Just as cortisol stimulates the activation of the fight/flight response, it also sends a signal to the hypothalamus and the pituitary to "chill out" and relax. This inhibits the production of CRF in the hypothalamus and the production of ACTH in the pituitary gland, resulting in stable levels of cortisol. This also results in a positive impact on your mood and anxiety.

Corticotropin-Releasing Factor (CRF): Produced by the hypothalamus and stimulates the pituitary gland to secrete adrenocorticotropic hormone (ACTH).

Adrenocorticotropic Hormone (ACTH): Secreted by the pituitary gland and stimulates the adrenal glands to increase production of mineralcorticoids and glucocorticoids. Cortisol is responsible for the majority of glucocorticoid activity.

APPENDIX III: GREEN SMOOTHIE RECIPES (BASIC FORMULA)

Leafy Greens (1 Cup)	**Liquid (1 Cup)**	**Assorted Fruit (1.5 Cups)**
Spinach	Water	Banana
Kale	Coconut Water	Apple
Romaine	Coconut Milk	Berries
Bok Choy	Almond Milk	Pineapple
Swiss Chard	Fresh Squeezed Juice	Grapes
Collards	*Cranberry Water	Pear
Dandelion		Peach
		Mango

*recipe below

Combine liquid with greens and pulse to pre-grind. Then add one scoop of vanilla whey protein powder + 2 tablespoons of flaxseed + 1 tablespoon of Agave (if desired). Add one, two, or three fruits of your choice to equal 1 ½ cups. Add 8 ice cubes. Blend on whole juice setting. Enjoy!

Cranberry Water—Makes 2 quarts: (I recommend drinking the entire amount each day.)

Add 8 ounces unsweetened cranberry juice (Lakewood 100% organic, Trader Joes, or Knudsen) to 56 ounces filtered water.

To make 1 cup: Mix 1 ounce of (2 tablespoons) unsweetened cranberry juice to 7 ounces of water.

Cranberry juice is a natural diuretic and packed with flavonoids, enzymes and organic acids such as malic acid, citric acid, and quinic acid which help to break down stubborn fat deposits in the lymphatic system—the body's "garbage collector" that transports all kinds of waste products not processed by the liver. Cranberry juice digests stagnated lymphatic wastes. Ann Louise Gittleman, a renowned nutritionist, recommends that you drink 2 quarts daily to help flush out water weight, balance blood sugar, improve cellulite and keep you liver and lymph in optimum cleansing mode.

Janet's Favorite Power Smoothie

- 1 cup almond milk (homemade is best)
- 1 cup packed spinach
- 1 scoop vanilla whey protein powder
- 2 tablespoons ground golden flaxseed
- 1 tablespoon Agave
- ½ cup strawberries
- ½ cup pineapple
- ½ banana
- 8 ice cubes

APPENDIX IV: SNACK IDEAS

If you're like me, it's sometimes difficult to come up with ideas for in-between meal snacks. Ideally, we should be eating three small meals per day with two additional snacks. Here are some suggestions for you to try.

½ cup Greek style yogurt with 2 tablespoons blueberries, raspberries, or strawberries

2 ounces (4 tablespoons) hummus with 1 cup sliced raw vegetables

1 cup mixed greens, 2 ounces sliced turkey or chicken, 1 tablespoon olive oil/apple cider vinegar dressing (2:1 ratio—2/3 tablespoon oil:1/3 tablespoon unfiltered apple cider vinegar (Trader Joes or Whole Foods)

1 unsweetened rice cake with 2 slices of avocado

1 unsweetened rice cake with 1 tablespoon almond or cashew butter

½ apple with 1 tablespoon almond or cashew butter

1 hardboiled egg and 10 almonds

2 ounces flaked salmon (fresh or canned) mixed with 1 tablespoon plain yogurt, squeeze of fresh lemon juice, salt and pepper. Serve on 6 crackers.

REFERENCES

Brizendine, L. (2006). *The female brain.* New York: Morgan Road Books.

Broughton. (1998). *Journal of Sleep Research, 1*, 166-178.

Burns, D. (1980). *Feeling good: The new mood therapy.* New York: Morrow.

Cunningham, J., Yonkers, K., O'Brien, S., & Eriksson, E. (2009). Update on research and treatment of premenstrual dysphoric disorder. *Harv Rev Psychiatry, 17*(2), 120-137.

Currier, M., & Nemeroff, C. (2014). Depression as a risk factor for cancer: From pathophysiological advances to treatment implications. *Annu Rev Med, 65*, 203-221.

Delarue, J., Matzinger, O., Binnert, C., Schneeiter, P., Chiolero, P., & Tappy, L. (2003). Fish oil prevents the adrenal activation elicited by mental stress in healthy men. *Diabetes Metab, 29*(3), 289-295.

Dinges, D., & Et al. (1997). Cumulative sleepiness, mood disturbance, and psychomotor vigilance performance decrements during a week of sleep restricted to 4-5 hours per night. *Sleep, 20*, 267-277.

Emmons, R., & McCullough, M. (2003). Counting blessings versus burden: An experimental investigation of gratitude and subjective well-being in daily life. *Journal of Personality and Social Psychology, 84*(2), 377-89.

Epel, E., Blackburn, E., Lin, J., Dhabhar, F., Adler, N., Morrow, J., & Cawthon, R. (2004). Accelerated telomere shortening in response to life stress. *Proceedings of the National Academy of Sciences of the United States of America, 101*(49), 17312-5.

Ferrari, E., Cravello, L., & Muzzoni, B. (2001). Age-related changes of the hypothalamic-pituitary-adrenal axis: Pathophysiological correlates. *Eur J Endocrinol, 144*(4), 319-329.

Fitzpatrick, L., Pace, C., & Wiita, B. (2000). Comparison of regimens containing oral micronized progesterone or medroxyprogesterone acetate on quality of life in postmenopausal women: A cross-sectional survey. *J Womens Health Gend Based Med., 9*(4), 381-7.

Graziottin, A., & Serafini, A. (2009). Depression and the menopause: Why antidepressants are not enough? *Menopause Int, 15*(2), 76-81.

Gutkowska, J., Janjowski, M., & Antunes-Rodrigues, J. (2014). Te role of oxytocin in cardiovascular regulation. *Braz J Med Biol Res, 47*(3), 206-14.

Holtorf, K. (2009). The bioidentical hormone debate: Are bioidentical hormones (estradiol, estriol, and progesterone) safe and more efficacious than commonly used synthetic versions in hormone replacement therapy? *Postgrad Med, 121*(1), 73-85.

Kelly, S., Davies, E., & Fearns, S. (2010). Effects of oral contraceptives containing ethinylestradiol with either drospirenone or levonorgestrel on various parameters associated with well-being in healthy women: A randomized single-blind, parallel group, multicentre study. *Clin Drug Investig, 30*, 326-336.

Kim, J., & Diamond, D. (2002). The stressed hippocampus, synaptic plasticity and lost memories. Nature Reviews Neuroscience, 3, 453-453.

Koenig, L., & Vaillant, G. (2009). A prospective study of church attendance and health over the lifespan. *Health Psychology, 28*(1), 117-24.

Lee, J., & Hopkins, V. (1996). *What your doctor may not tell you about menopause: The breakthrough book on natural progesterone.* New York: Warner Books.

Lin, P., & Su, K. (2007). A meta-analytic review of double-blind, placebo-controlled trials of antidepressant efficacy of omega-3 fatty acids. *J Clinical Psychiatry, 68*(7), 1056-1061.

Lucchetti, G., Lucchetti, A., & Koenig, H. (2011). Impact of spirituality/religiosity on mortality: Comparison with other health interventions. *Explore, 7*(4), 234-8.

McCullough, M., Hoyt, W., Larson, D., Koenig, H., & Thoresen, C. (2000).

Religious involvement and mortality: A meta-analytic review. *Health Psychology, 19*(3), 211-222.

Medina, J. (2008). *Brain Rules* (pp. 169-195). Seattle: Pear Press.

Moses-Kolko, E., Berga, S., & Kairo, B. (2009). Transdermal estradiol for postpartum depression: A promising treatment option. *Clin Obstet Gynecol, 52*, 516-529.

New Findings on Sleep Disorders and CAM. (2006, September 18). Retrieved September 9, 2014, from http://nccam.nih.gov/research/results/spotlight/090106.htm

Parry, B. (2008). Perimenopausal depression. *Am J Psychiatry, 165*, 23-27.

Pearlstein, T., & Steiner, M. (2008). Premenstrual dysphoric disorder: Burden of illness and treatment update. *J Psychiatry Neurosci, 33*(4), 291-301.

Pluchino, N., Cubeddu, A., & Giannini, A. (2009). Progestogens and brain: An update. *Maturitas, 62*, 349-355.

Raison, C. (2014, July 15). Mind-Body Neurobiology of Depression. Retrieved August 20, 2014, from http://www.psychcongress.com/neurobiology

Ratney, J. (2008). *Spark, The Revolutionary New Science of Exercise and the Brain.* New York: Little Brown & Company.

Reiss, U., & Zucker, M. (2001). *Natural hormone balance for women: Look younger, feel stronger, and live life with exuberance.* New York: Pocket Books.

Rovio, S., & Et al. (2005). Leisure-time physical activity at midlife and the risk of dementia and Alzheimer's disease. *Lancet Neurology, 4*, 705-711.

Russell, D. (1996). The UCLA Loneliness Scale (Version 3): Reliability, validity, and factor structure. *Journal of Personality Assessment, 66*, 20-40.

Schabus, M., Hodlmoser, K., Pecherstorfer, T., & Klosch, G. (2005). Influence of midday naps on declarative memory performance and motivation. *Somnologie, 9*, 148-148.

Schmidt, P., & Rubinow, D. (2009). Sex hormones and mood in the perimenopause. *Ann N Y Acad Sci, 1179*, 70-85.

Skarupski, K., Tangney, C., Li, H., Ouyang, B., Evans, D., & Morris, M.

(2010). Longitudinal association of vitamin B-6, folate, and vitamin B-12 with depressive symptoms among older adults over time. *American Journal of Clinical Nutrition, 92*(2), 330-335.

Smedes, L. (1984). *Forgive and forget: Healing the hurts we don't deserve.* San Francisco: Harper & Row.

Southwick, S., & Charney, D. (2012). *Resilience: The science of mastering life's greatest challenges.* New York: Cambridge University Press.

Stahl, S. (2008). *Stahl's essential psychopharmacology: Neuroscientific basis and practical applications* (3rd ed.). Cambridge: Cambridge University Press.

Taylor, S., Klein, L., Lewis, B., Gruenewald, T., Gurung, R., & Updegraff, J. (2000). Biobehavioral Responses to Stress in Females: Tend-and-Befriend, Not Fight-or-Flight. *Psychological Review, 107*(3), 411-429.

Toussaint, L., Owen, A., & Cheadle, A. (2012). Forgive to live: Forgiveness, health, and longevity. *Journal of Behavioral Medicine, 35*(4), 375-86.

University of Chicago. (2009, February 19). Loneliness Affects How The Brain Operates. Retrieved October 29, 2014, from http://www.sciencedaily.com/releases/2009/02/090215151800.htm

Verghese, J., & Et al. (2003). Leisure activities and the risk of dementia in the elderly. *New England Journal of Medicine, 348*, 2508-2516.

Wales, J. (2012). Disordered pubertal development. *Arch Dis Child Educ Pract Ed, 97*, 9-16.

Warren, R. (2014, May 14). Retrieved January 6, 2015, from http://rickwarren.org/devotional/english/the-definition-of-joy

Williams, A., Cotter, A., Sabina, A., Girard, C., Goodman, J., & Katz, D. (2004). The role for vitamin B-6 as treatment for depression: A systematic review. *Family Practice, 22*(5), 532-37.

Wise, D., Felker, A., & Stahl, S. (2008). Tailoring treatment of depression for women across the reproductive lifecycle: The importance of pregnancy, vasomotor symptoms, and other estrogen-related events in psychopharmacology. *CNS Spectr, 13*(8), 647-662.

Wise, J. (2009). Cognitive-behavioral therapy versus usual clinical care for youth depression: An initial test of transportability to community clinics and clinicians. *J Consult Clin Psychol, 77*(3), 383-396.

ABOUT THE AUTHOR

Janet R. Leathem PMHNP, BC is a graduate of Columbia University in New York City and is a board certified psychiatric nurse practitioner with over 35 years of success helping others achieve personal wellness.

She is an evangelical Christian, a results driven therapist, a visionary healthcare administrator, and a dynamic seminar leader who has been called to share her expertise with others.